CLASSICAL STUDIES

Law

ouns and Postpositives in Attic Prose
ation of Aeneas

SCOTTISH

1: D. M. MacDowell, *Spartan*
2: P. B. Corbett, *The Scurra*
3: M. H. B. Marshall, *Verbs,*
4: C. J. Mackie, *The Character*

SCOTTISH CLASSICAL STUDIES

THE SCURRA

by

PHILIP CORBETT

SCOTTISH ACADEMIC PRESS

EDINBURGH

Published by
Scottish Academic Press Ltd
33 Montgomery Street, Edinburgh EH7 5JX

SBN 7073 0475 X

British Library Cataloguing in Publication Data

Corbett, Philip
    The Scurra.—(Scottish Classical Studies; 2)
    1. Fools and jesters   2. Names, Latin
    I. Title   II. Series
    790.2   GT3670

    ISBN 0-7073-0475-X

Printed in Great Britain by
Clark Constable, Edinburgh and London

Contents

The author wishes to thank Professor MacDowell and Professor Walsh for accepting these exploratory observations on the *scurra* in the new series Scottish Classical Studies, and for their helpful advice and salutary correction of the manuscript. Mr Jeffreys-Powell also made many valuable criticisms and suggestions for which I am indebted. Finally, Professor MacDowell read the proofs with great care, correcting much that I might have missed.

I

A Problem of Identity

The *scurra* is a rather puzzling figure. He is described throughout Latin literature as *urbanus* and *dicax*, but also as *mimicus* and then again as *saltator* and as *ioculator*. These epithets clearly indicate that the *scurra* is an entertainer, in effect a mime performer and, furthermore, one not only proficient in dance ritual interpretation but also possessing a vocal repertory of *iocularia*, as Prudentius neatly sums it up in his *Crowns of Martyrdom* — the Roman Prefect is rebuking the martyr Saint Laurence:

> *impune tantas, furcifer,*
> *strophas cavillo mimico*
> *te nexuisse existimas,*
> *dum, scurra, saltas fabulam?*

Do you suppose, you scoundrel,
that you can get away with contriving
such a display of the mime-jester's
art and your dancing clown's act?
(*Peristeph.*2.317f.)

However, numerous contexts show him, not as an entertainer but as an individual of restless temperament, a ne'er-do-well spendthrift, a malicious gossip and scandal-monger, in fact a sinister figure — *opprobria fingere saevus* (Horace, *Ep.*1.15.10), rather than *deliciae popli* (Plautus, *Most.*15).

The late Imperial glossaries define the *scurra* (*scur, scurro, scurrio*) as *parasitus buccellarius* ("loud-mouth"), *subtilis impostor* ("illusionist", "conjuror"), *irrisor* ("mocking jester") etc., among other expressions denoting greed or lechery; Greek terms employed include εὔστομος ("flatterer"), γελωτοποιός ("laughter-maker"), εὐτράπελος ("wit"), σκώπτης ("jester") (see *Corp.Gloss.Lat.*II, pp. 180 and 592; IV, p. 390). These various definitions suggest the parasite entertainer who exercises his wit alternatively in flattery of the host and guests, and in malicious gossip against absent acquaintance as well as performing the conjuror and clown.

The main obstacle to a complete understanding of the *scurra* is our ignorance of what his name really means. Its derivation has never been precisely established. The spelling *scur* suggests a connection with σκῶρ and σκωρία in the sense of "refuse", "trash", "ordure". The Latin derivative *scoria* (*scuria*) is glossed as *sordes metallorum* and *quod de ferro cadit* (*CGL*V.243, 21 and 22) and cf. *stercus ferri* "dross", "slag", while the cognate *scorio* is glossed as *stultus fatuus* (ibid. 610, 44) and *scories* as *stulti stolidi fatui* (ibid. 614, 54), both obvious echoes of Plt. *Bacch.* 1088-9 Nic: *stulti, stolidi, fatui, fungi, bardi, blenni, buccones,/solus ego omnis longe antideo stultitia et moribus indoctis* — 'I outstrip in stupidity and ignorant behaviour all these stupid dullard fools, these slow-witted blockhead babblers'. It would seem then from these examples that *scurra* has a meaning similar to *nugator* "trifler", "jester" and to *nugae* itself, which has a similar basic meaning of "trash", "scourings" etc., but in its normal figurative sense = *ineptiae* (cf. *nugas agere*) and even *inepti homines* (cf. Cic. *Att.*6.3.5 *amicos habet meras nugas* — "he has friends who are pure trash").

On the other hand, the *scurra* is a *saltator* and so a connection with the Greek root σκιρ-, as in σκαίρω, σκιρτάω, σκίρτος etc., is not impossible. The satyroi — the goat-men dancing chorus of Greek parody drama, known for their *dicacitas* (malicious wit, and cf. Hor. *A.P.* 225 *satyri dicaces*), are called σκίρτοι and σκιρτοπόδαι ("skittish"). At first sight the connection seems even likely but, if *scurra* simply means a dancer of mime, then the name is inadequate to render the character's mischief-making vocal accomplishment.

Forcellini, *Lexicon* II, p. 505 s.v. equates the *scurra* with the βωμολόχος, *qui risum ab audientibus captat dictis iocularibus vel corporis gestu, non habita ratione verecundiae aut dignitatis* — a vulgar jester and mimic; but the *scurra*'s parasitic function sometimes led to erroneous derivations like Isidore's *Etym.* 10.255 *scurra, qui sectari quempiam solet cibi gratia. A sequendo igitur scurras appellatos.* — the *scurra* who will follow after anyone at all for the sake of food — *scurrae* are therefore so called from their practice of "following".

Ernout-Meillet, *Dict. Etym.* p. 912, describes the *scurra* as "citadin" and "galant débauché", but does not supply a derivation. Max Niedermann, *Hist. Lautl. des Lateinischen* p. 124, compares the geminated consonant of *scurra* with that characteristic of the names of Atellan farce — *bucco, maccus, pappus, dossennus* (to which one may perhaps add *cicirrus*) and of nicknames like *flaccus, gibber, lippus, varro* and *vappa* — possibly dialectal importations of Etruscan or Oscan origin.

Cicero has an interesting remark in *De Natura Deorum*. He is commenting on the contempt Epicurus professed to have for the theological systems of the Platonists and the Stoics. His followers Phaedrus and Zeno emulated the master and *Zeno quidem non eos solum qui tum erant Apollodorum Silum ceteros figebat maledictis sed Socratem ipsum parentem philosophiae Latino verbo utens scurram Atticum fuisse dicebat.* (1.93)

I do not think Zeno meant that Socrates was a clown or jester, still less a mime player, but that he was a busy-body, know-all and public nuisance, which is exactly how the *scurra* is described in Plautus and Horace and is incidentally a more apposite criticism of the Father of Philosophy. Two points — the expression *figere maledictis* proves that the term *scurra* was an insult, not a compliment; Cicero remarks that *scurra* is a Latin word (*Latino verbo utens*) which simply means that for him it was not known to be of Greek origin and that Zeno did not use some Greek equivalent.

Macrobius in his *Saturnalia* cites a number of Cicero's own mordant witticisms, for instance the remark on his son-in-law Lentulus, a man of short stature who appeared wearing a long sword — "Who has tied my son-in-law to a sword?", and tells us that Cicero was commonly called the consular *scurra* (*Sat.*2.1.12 and 2.3).

The clue to the apparent paradox of the *scurra*'s personality, now pleasing entertainer, now social menace, lies in a twofold identity. On the one hand we find the professional mime player, endowed with a variety of skills but best known for his malicious tongue; on the other the amateur man about town, city wit and scandal-monger whose chief characteristic also is malicious intent.

This twofold identity has not been discerned by scholars who have spoken about the *scurra* — in particular Otto Ribbeck in his "Agroikos" (= *Abhandl. d. sächs. Gesells. d. Wissenschaften, phil.-hist. Kl.*, Bd. 10, pp. 55-66) and Paul Lejay in his *Oeuvres d'Horace* vol. 2, 1911, pp. 551 f. The latter remarks "le mot *scurra* désigne un genre de vie, non pas un caractère", which is only a half-truth. For examples of the word, the reader may best consult Pauly-Wissowa *RE* s.v., Forcellini's *Lexicon* and the OCD s.v.

II

The Professional Jester in Plautus

Before considering the *scurra* as he is first mentioned in
Roman literature, in the plays of Plautus, it is relevant to say a
word about the parasite characters of Roman comedy, none
of whom are themselves *scurrae*. For certain of these parasites
are professional jesters and therefore call for comparison
with the actual *scurra*, the jester par excellence in later Roman
tradition, both pagan and Christian.

To turn to the Greek world; the parasite was a stock
character of Greek social comedy and obviously designed to
provoke amusement. Athenaeus (ca. A.D. 200) of Naucratis,
an important Greek settlement on the Egyptian delta,
claimed familiarity with hundreds of Greek plays and his
literary symposium, the *Deipnosophistae*, is an invaluable
source of extracts from Middle and New Comedy writers
illustrating the parasite's role. From these we can see that the
parasites of Roman comedy are modelled upon those of the
Greek world, some of whom were real personages, mentioned by several authors in more than one of their plays.
Among them were Tithymallus (the Purge) who figured in
Alexis, Antiphanes and Timocles; Corydos (the Lark), whose
real name was Eucrates, mentioned in Alexis and Timocles;
Philoxenos who was called Pternokopis (Ham-Cleaver) ap-
pearing in Axionicus, Menander and Machon, and the
notorious Chaerephon who was found in Menander, Timocles, Antiphanes, Diphilus, Apollodorus and others
(Athen.6.239f-246b).

Athenaeus tells us that, for the Greeks, the parasite was essentially a flatterer, harking back to Old Comedy, for Eupolis had a play "The Flatterers" (*Colaces*), named from its chorus (Athen.6.236e). But the flatterer must also be a wit (χαρίεις — *festivus, lepidus*) or be thrown out of doors — ibid. 236f ἐπὶ δεῖπνον ἐρχόμεσθα—οὗ δεῖ χαρίεντα πολλὰ τὸν κόλακ' εὐθέως λέγειν ἢ 'κφέρεται θύραζε. Before Eupolis there was the Sicilian Epicharmus, whose "Hope or Wealth" presents a parasite whose function is to be witty, make much laughter and praise his host — ibid. 235f χαρίης τ' εἰμὶ καὶ ποιέω πόλυν γέλωτα καὶ τὸν ἱστιῶντ' ἐπαινέω.

It is true that Chaireas in Menander's *Dyscolos* hardly meets these requirements. He is, as Eric Handley remarks (*The Dyskolos of Menander*, p. 140), more of a lover's confidential aide, with something of the hanger-on and flatterer, rather than the hungry and sharp-witted entertainer (and see also F. H. Sandbach in *Menander, a Commentary*, pp. 131-2). The distinction is made between entertainer and mere flatterer by Gnatho in Terence's *Eunuchus*, who is based upon Struthias the soldier's servant in Menander's *Colax*.

Much more representative of the parasite-entertainer is Philip the "Laughter-maker" (γελωτοποιός) whom we meet in Xenophon's *Symposium* and who jokes as soon as the host's door is opened, and tries to keep up the performance, only to meet with considerable coolness until the ice is eventually melted by his persistent efforts — *Symp.* 1.11: συνεσ-κευασμένος τε παρεῖναι ἔφη πάντα τἀπιτήδεια — ὥστε δειπνεῖν τἀλλότρια, καὶ τὸν παῖδα δὲ ἔφη πάνυ πιέζεσθαι διά τε τὸ φέρειν μηδὲν καὶ διὰ τὸ ἀνάριστον εἶναι — he declared he had come all prepared to dine on — someone else's fare, and that his boy was much burdened with carrying — nothing, and with having had no breakfast.

Philip also does imitations, burlesquing the performance

of a dancing boy and girl (2.22); he is thus a *saltator/ioculator* like the Roman *scurra*. He is questioned as to why he takes such pride in his profession (τί ὁρῶν ἐν τῇ γελωτοποιίᾳ μέγα ἐπ᾽ αὐτῇ φρονοίη — 4.50). He replies that he has every right, for everyone knows him to be a jester and when they can afford it, they invite him, but avoid him in misfortune lest they should be compelled to laugh in spite of themselves — φεύγουσιν ἀμεταστρεπτί, φοβούμενοι μὴ καὶ ἄκοντες γελάσωσι.

The parasite of Greek comedy is a flatterer and a wit, the forbear of those we find in Roman comedy. It is apparent also that the parasite in Greek society was a real life personage. When we examine the professional jester-parasite as presented in Roman comedy we get the same impression. But not all the parasites in Roman comedy belong to this class. Looking at the nine parasites of Plautus and the two of Terence, we discern from the nature of the role they play that they fall into distinct categories, although of course all display the comic parasites' characteristics of impudence, ready wit and perpetual hunger. I would distinguish four such groups, one only of which comprises the professional jesters mentioned above. These last alone are important for this investigation and I mention the other three groups merely to dispose of them. They are as follows:

1. The Parasite Protagonist

Plautus' Curculio and Terence's Phormio play the leading role in the plays to which they give their name. Their supreme self-confidence, courage and ingenuity fit them to be the masters of the intrigue. They display in fact the same qualities as the *servi callidi* who, like Palaestrio of the *Miles* and Epidicus and Pseudolus in the plays named after them, are the heroes of the action. So much so that one feels that

Plautus must have hesitated as to whether the slave or the parasite should be the chief exponent of his humour. Indeed, Curculio is mistaken for a slave and behaves exactly like a *servus currens* (*Curc.* 280f.).

Since we have Terence's Phormio as well as Plautus' Curculio, it is likely that the parasite protagonist of *palliatae* is derived from Greek New Comedy. The title of Menander's *Colax* implies that a parasite flatterer is prominent in the play and we have noted above that the Old Comedy writer Eupolis had a play called *The Flatterers*.

2. The Soldier's Parasite

Three of the parasites in Roman comedy are the attendants of a well-known type of farcical character, the boastful soldier. They are Artotrogus of the *Miles*, an unnamed parasite in the service of Cleomachus in the *Bacchides*, and Terence's Gnatho, the servant of Thraso in the *Eunuchus*. The first two play insignificant parts. Indeed, Artotrogus appears only in the single, long scene which constitutes the first Act of the *Miles*. He is merely a foil for Pyrgopolynices, answering his outrageous boasting with equally outrageous flattery. This character Artotrogus may be derived from the *Colax* of Menander. Act I of the *Miles* is separated from the rest of the play by the Prologue, which follows instead of preceding it, as usually and normally. If it is so derived, then Plautus decided against giving Artotrogus the leading role in his play, assigning this instead to the boastful soldier, thus conforming to the model for the rest of the play, the *Alazon* (Braggart) of unknown authorship. This is consistent with his making the soldier's parasite an insignificant part in the *Bacchides* also.

On the other hand, Terence was accused of plagiarism by his rival Lanuvinus on the occasion of a rehearsal of the

Eunuchus (Prol.25f.), for taking the parts of the soldier and his parasite from *Colax* plays by Naevius and Plautus. Terence denied the charge, declaring that the characters in question were taken from Menander's *Colax* and that he knew nothing of the Latin versions (*ea ex fabula factas prius Latinas scisse sese, id vero pernegat* — Prol.33-34). Whether there was truth in his denials or not, the fact emerges that Menander, Naevius and Plautus were all credited with plays in which the soldier's flatterer was given a leading role.

Cleomachus' parasite appears for even less time, in two brief scenes at the beginning of Act IV of the *Bacchides*, to run an errand for the Captain. A couple of jokes and he is gone. Anonymous himself, he despises his master — *parasitus ego sum hominis nequam atque improbi* — "I am the parasite of a worthless and wicked man" (573).

Clearly then, Plautus is not prepared to develop this type of parasite, who is merely an abject flatterer — Art. *adsentandumst quidquid hic mentibitur* — "I must agree with whatever this fellow shall invent" (*Miles* 35). Such an insignificant creature cannot make a protagonist like Curculio.

Turning to Terence, we find the soldier's parasite Gnatho. He too is a mere flatterer. He comes briefly to life when he explains his philosophy to an acquaintance, and his remarks on this occasion are important. I shall return to him.

3. The Hired Trickster

There are two more nameless parasites in Plautus. The first is in the *Asinaria* and, like the one in the *Bacchides*, appears late in the play. His role is to draw up a written agreement between Diabolus' girl and the procuress. He appears again in Act V.2 as an informer, revealing to Artemona the misconduct of her husband and son. Such a role puts him into the category of *sycophanta*, informer, trickster, rogue in general.

The other appears in Act IV.2 of the *Trinummus* and is actually referred to as a *sycophanta* in the *dramatis personae*. Despite his late appearance, special importance attaches to him, for he confers upon the play its title — *huic ego die nomen Trinummo faciam: nam ego operam meam tribus nummis hodie locavi ad artis nugatorias* (843-4) — "To this day I will give the name 'Three Quid', for I have this day for three quid hired out my services in the arts of mischief". For these *nugae*, deception and intrigue, his qualifications are that he is *mendacilocum, falsidicum, confidentem* (769), traits which of course he shares with all the parasites of comedy, as with the *servi callidi*. Indeed, the three categories I have used serve to distinguish the degrees of importance or lack of it which the characters mentioned assume, rather than to refine upon their individuality. The *sycophanta* of the *Trinummus* is a *nugator* 'trickster'; so is Curculio, and both terms mean the same thing in comedy. The stage-manager(*choragus*), referring to Curculio, declares (462) *edepol nugatorem lepidum lepide hunc nactust Phaedromus, halophantum an sycophantam magis esse dicam nescio* — "Phaedromus has got himself a smart joker in this fellow. I don't know whether to call him a deceiver or a deceptionist", and he fears for the safety of the costume he has rented to him for the part — *ornamenta quae locavi metuo ut possim recipere* (464). Similarly, the *sycophanta* in *Trinummus* remarks that his employer *ornamenta a chorago haec sumpsit suo periculo* (858) — "He has hired this costume of mine from the manager at his own risk."

All the parasites mentioned above doubtless derive from Greek comedy models. Only Curculio is developed by Plautus with the zest he bestows upon the creation of his slave protagonists. George Duckworth remarks in his *The Nature of Roman Comedy* p. 265 that "the parasite is the funny man *par excellence* of Roman comedy", and yet Plautus invests the slave with the hilarious role of cunning confidant to a far greater extent. Probably the incongruity of making the slave, normally so subdued a figure in Roman society, into an important intriguer appealed to him.

We may now pass on to our fourth category of parasite, one which, to my mind, is given by Plautus peculiar and, perhaps, topical significance.

4. The *Parasitus Ridiculus*

We now come to a group of parasites who are not masters of intrigue like Curculio and Phormio or simply confidential agents like the nameless parasite in the *Asinaria*; nor are they *sycophantae*, hired for specific purposes of mischief (*artes nugatoriae*), like the one in the *Trinummus*, nor again simply flatterers like Artotrogus or Cleomachus' servant in the *Bacchides*. The group in question are by calling professional jesters, whose main task is to amuse their patrons by entertaining them with *dicta ridicula*. I call them therefore *parasiti ridiculi*.

This category does not appear in Terence. Plautus has three parasites who refer to their stock in trade of *dicta*, Gelasimus of the *Stichus*, Ergasilus of the *Captivi* and Saturio of the *Persa*. To their number it is tempting to add a fourth, Peniculus of the *Menaechmi*, by virtue of his name and the manner in which it is bestowed. It would seem that these characters, as presented by Plautus, are essentially Roman, part of the background of his day. It is true that they play a part in the action, sometimes a fairly important one, although nothing approaching the leading role of a Curculio, and no doubt their parts originate in a Greek model. But, in their capacity as professional jesters as opposed to mere witty flatterers, I think they are also part of the Roman scene and that this is borne out in the remarks they make, particularly at the outset of the plays in which they appear.

First, Gelasimus, whose very name implies that he is a "laughter man". In true parasite style, his opening remark at the beginning of Act I, scene 3 (*Stich.* 155f.) is: "I suspect that Hunger herself was my Mother, for ever since I was born I have never had my fill." The first dozen lines or so enlarge in humorous vein upon this theme. No doubt there was material for these remarks in the Greek model.

But what follows (171f.) is, I feel, Plautus' innovation: *nunc si ridiculum hominem quaerat quispiam, venalis ego sum cum ornamentis omnibus* — "if anyone should be looking for a jester, I am for sale with all my equipment". What these *ornamenta* are, we shall shortly discover. Having already the cue in the reference to a Mother, Plautus now improvises with a Father! *Gelasimo nomen mi indidit parvo pater, quia inde iam a pausillo puero ridiculus fui* (174) — "My father gave me the name Gelasimus when I was small, because right from being a tiny tot I have been a joker." Poverty was the reason for his becoming an object of mirth, for she teaches the tricks of the trade to all she touches upon.

However, it is not easy to earn one's victuals nowadays since invitations to dine have fallen off — *oratio una interiit hominum pessume . . . qua ante utebantur: 'veni illo ad cenam . . .'* (183f.). This statement is important, for it is echoed by the other *parasiti ridiculi*, and may be not merely a typical comic discomfiture appropriate to *palliatae* but may also have a topical significance for the jester *métier* at Rome. Reluctance to invite people to dinner is of course a standing joke with the Romans. Daemones at the end of the *Rudens* turns to the audience and says "Spectators, I would invite you also to dinner, if I didn't suppose you were invited already" (1418-1420). Simo in the *Pseudolus* (1330) says "Why don't you invite the spectators too?", and Pseudolus replies "They never invite me, so I won't them".

Another significant remark is made by Gelasimus (198f.): *sed curiosi sunt hic complures mali, alienas res qui curant studio maximo, quibus ipsis nullast res, quam procurent, sua* — "Now there are a lot of inquisitive malicious types hereabouts [i.e. at Rome] who concern themselves with other people's business, having none of their own to look after." This complaint we are also to hear voiced by others in relevant contexts, which we shall consider in due course.

All that Gelasimus can do is to bewail the vanished splendour of bygone meals. The eavesdropping maid Crocotium remarks that he is never so funny as when he is hungry — *ridiculus aeque nullus est quando esurit* (217). He is reduced to such straits that he must hold an auction and sell his joke books — *logos ridiculos vendo* (221). They are second to none and consist of jestings, flatterings and little travesties of truth — *cavillationes, adsentatiunculas ac perieratiunculas parasiticas*, the stock in trade of the professional jester. Not only these will he dispose of, but also his *ornamenta*, his rusty *strigil* and flask. These too are professional items, as we see confirmed in the remarks of another *ridiculus*, Saturio of the *Persa* (120f.).

Crocotium decides to accost him; "Good morning, Gelasimus" she says. "That is not my name" he replies. "For sure it *was* your name." "It was indeed, but it has been my experience to lose it [*fuit disertim, verum id usu perdidi*]. Now I am called by my true name Miccotrogus [Nibblecrumb]" (242). Compare this name with that of Artotrogus (Nibbleloaf) of the *Miles*.

Here I think we have a clue to Plautus' procedure with this as with his other parasite jesters. Miccotrogus was possibly the name of the parasite in his Greek model. In adapting his role to that of a professional jester to befit a Romanized scene,

he changed the name to the evocative Gelasimus, meant to
suggest γελωτοποιός.

At the good news of Epignomus' (the young master)
arrival (372), Gelasimus decides not to sell his jest-books
(*logi*) after all (383). But Epignomus has brought back some
parasite funny-men with him from overseas, so in despair he
must put them up again for sale. Meantime, he will swot up
some of his best *mots* to try to get the better of the newcomers
— *ibo intro ad libros et discam de dictis melioribus* (400). Here then
is a clear reference to the *libri* or *dicta ridicula* which are the
stock in trade of the professional jester parasite.

At the beginning of Act III.2 Gelasimus is in good heart —
*libros inspexi; tam confido quam potis, me meum optenturum regem
ridiculis meis* (454) — "I've had a look at my books and I'm
sure as sure that I can hold on to my patron with my funny
remarks." He cadges an invitation from Epignomus, declaring he is a humble fellow, ready to sit at the lowest bench —
*hau postulo equidem med in lecto accumbere: scis tu me esse imi subselli
virum* (488-9). The remark is echoed by Ergasilus (*Capt.*471)
nil morantur iam Lacones imi subselli viros. I prefer *imi subselli*
to the doubtful Latin *unisubselli* favoured by Leo. But Epignomus decides against inviting him in the company of
important envoys from Ambracia. In desperation he tries
Pamphilippus, Epignomus' brother, who has however promised to dine out. This is the end for Gelasimus, who quits
the play with the bitter remark *viden ridiculos nihili fieri, atque
ipsos parasitarier?* (634) — "Don't you see how jesters are held
of no account and the masters themselves turn parasite?"

Thus all his attempts at earning meals with the aid of his
witty repertoire are frustrated, in a situation where patrons
no longer care about jesters and prefer to dine out. I
underline this situation because it is repeated in the case of
Ergasilus and alluded to by Saturio and by the soldier's

parasite Gnatho of Terence's *Eunuchus*.

It is to be noted that the slave Stichus, who gives his name to the play in which Gelasimus appears early on (I.3), does not himself appear until Act III and that he enjoys a favour denied to the parasite. Plautus' predilection for the slave role is obvious in most of his work and of course in the context Stichus has been given the day off to celebrate Epignomus' and his own safe home-coming from abroad (422). But the allocation of seventy-eight lines of monologue to Gelasimus on his first appearance compels an attention to him out of all proportion to the defeatist and defeated role he is to perform. Plautus is thus drawing our interest to the person and his calling much more than to his dramatic role.

We may now turn to Ergasilus, who appears at the beginning of Act I of the *Captivi*, in a monologue of forty lines, showing the importance Plautus wishes to attach to this personage also, and again this importance is hardly in keeping with the part he plays in the action. Moreover, he is not mentioned in the preceding Prologue.

We have seen that Gelasimus had his jester name conferred upon him by his Father — *Gelasimo nomen mi indidit parvo pater* (*Stich.*174). Ergasilus' opening remark is *Iuventus nomen indidit Scorto mihi, eo quia invocatus soleo esse in convivio* — "The Young Men have conferred the name Mistress upon me, because I am generally called upon at dinner parties." There is a double play on words here — *invocatus* can mean "invited" or "invoked" as one's mistress (*scortum*) is invoked (for luck) in a dice game. *Esse* can mean "to eat" as well as "to be present". Such clever word play is in keeping with the jester role.

To my mind, the term *Iuventus* evokes a Roman context. These Young Men are not the individuals of New Comedy but a collective group, and Ergasilus is not referring to his normal patron, Philopolemus, who is a prisoner of war, away from home. Indeed, Philopolemus' generosity is contrasted with the selfish indifference of the unnamed *Iuventus*: *nam nulla est spes iuventutis, sese omnes amant; ille demum* [Philopolemus] *antiquis est adulescens moribus, cuius numquam voltum tranquillavi gratis* (114-115) — "There is no hope from the Young Men, they love only themselves; he only is a lad of the old sort. I never smoothed his brow without reward." The Young Men are in fact *derisores* (71), inclined to make fun of Ergasilus, not to feed him, so that his plight is exactly that of Gelasimus at *Stich.*183: *oratio una interiit . . . 'veni illo ad cenam'*.

I suggested above that the name Gelasimus was Plautus' own invention. What of the name Ergasilus, rendered into Scortum ('mistress', 'whore') by the jesting Young Men? It is almost an anagram of Gelasimus! Plautus I think meant it to suggest the Greek *ergasimos*, literally 'workable', but applied to prostitutes as working upon their backs, as in Artemidorus, *Onirocriticon* I.78: καὶ γὰρ πρός τινων ἐργάσιμοι λέγονται (sc. ἑταῖραι), καὶ οὐδὲν ἀρνησάμεναι παρέχουσιν ἑαυτάς — 'Indeed prostitutes are called "work-mates" by some: they offer themselves, refusing nothing.'

Quasi mures semper edimus alienum cibum (77) — "like mice we are always eating other people's food" remarks bitterly our jester, exactly the same words used by his fellow *ridiculus* Saturio at *Persa* 58. He enlarges upon this and then angrily bursts out: *et hic quidem hercle, nisi qui colaphos perpeti potest parasitus frangique aulas in caput, ire extra portam Trigeminam ad saccum licet* (88-90) — "here by god [at Rome of course] unless a parasite can endure clouts and the breaking of pots on his head, he might as well go out at Three Arch Gate [near the Aventine Hill] and take a portering job". Clearly Plautus is presenting us with a Roman jester, the clown who is everyone's butt, the counterpart of those we meet in medieval times at the Court of King and Bishop.

His next monologue is also a long one, the thirty-six lines which constitute Act III, scene 1. He laments his hungry condition and concludes (469f.) "The parasitic art can go to the devil" — *ita iuventus iam ridiculos inopesque ab se segregat. Nil morantur iam Lacones imi subselli viros, plagipatidas* — "the Young Men now fend off the funny-men and the men without means. No longer do they care about the Spartan heroes of the lowest bench, the slap-happy." *Ipsi obsonant, quae parasitorum ante erat provincia . . . neque ridiculos iam terrunci faciunt, sese omnes amant* — "the masters themselves do the shopping, which before was the parasites' province, and no longer care a brass farthing for the funny-men, loving themselves alone" — the last three words an echo of 104.

Here then is another clear statement of the decline of the professional parasite jester, due to his abandonment by the Young Men, who are all in collusion like the oil merchants in the Velabrum (another Roman touch) — *omnes de compecto rem agunt, quasi in Velabro olearii* (489).

From now on Ergasilus fares better than did Gelasimus. He appears again in Act IV and has lively exchanges with the old man Hegio. He renders service by bringing good news and is rewarded with culinary bliss. His conduct now resembles the cheerful impudence of Plautus' slave heroes, and the fact is that his creator ceases to think and treat of him as a *ridiculus*. Having drawn attention to the jester in decline in the early part of the play, he now lets the subject drop, reverting one feels to the parasite character as presented in his Greek model. The hard-hearted *Iuventus* are also of course no longer mentioned.

But, turning to the *Menaechmi* and to Peniculus, we find them again. Just as we are bound to link Ergasilus with Gelasimus, through the similarity of the sentiments they express regarding their status as *ridiculi*, so we must link

Peniculus with Ergasilus, because both are presented to us in precisely the same way. Ergasilus opens the *Captivi* with the words *Iuventus nomen indidit Scorto mihi* . . .; Peniculus opens the *Menaechmi* with the words *Iuventus nomen fecit Peniculo mihi, ideo quia mensam, quando edo, detergeo* — "The Young Men made the name Peniculus (Little Brush) for me, because, when I eat, I sweep the table." This time Plautus has chosen a Latin word for the name of his funny-man, but one which, like Ergasilus, has a lascivious connotation, for Peniculus can also mean Little Penis. This form of presentation (*Iuventus nomen indidit*) recalls the Greek, as in Antiphanes' *The Ancestors* where the parasite remarks καλοῦσί μ᾽ οἱ νεώτεροι — σκηπτόν — "the Young Men call me 'Whizzkid'" (because of his many talents) — Athen. 6.238e.

However, in spite of this opening to a thirty-two line monologue, Peniculus is not presented to us as a professional jester. He does not refer to himself as a *ridiculus*, nor does he talk of his jest-books. Instead, Plautus develops him simply as a conventional greedy parasite, eager to perform services in the hope of a meal. He speaks enthusiastically of his patron Menaechmus, as did Ergasilus of Philopolemus, though he too mentions that invitations have fallen off, but without blaming the *Iuventus* as responsible for the neglect. Our impression of him is as a gluttonous dependant and obsequious flatterer, although a humorous one, for he has many witty exchanges with Menaechmus and Erotium. In fact, he admits to being an *assentator* (yes man). In response to Menaechmus' "What do you say to this?" (162), he replies "Indeed, anything you want me to, to this I say Yes or I say No" — *id enim quod tu vis, id aio atque id nego*. This remark I consider important as indicating the decline of the professional parasite jester in the Rome of Plautus' day, equipped with a repertory of jest-books, like Gelasimus and Ergasilus, and whose art should earn him a place in the dining room, albeit at the "lowest bench", to the humiliating status of abject flatterer and errand boy. Such is Peniculus in the *Menaechmi* and Plautus shows him at 667 as defeated and rejected by both Menaechmus and his wife, who have no further use for his services — *ex hac familia me plane excidisse intellego*. There is no doubt that, like Galasimus and Ergasilus, he resents his situation. For Peniculus is a man of spirit, as witness his angry outburst with Menaechmus/Sosicles, whom he mistakes for his twin, for abandoning him in the forum and losing him his lunch (486f.).

For this bold conjecture regarding the jester's loss of status I find confirmation in Terence. Turning to the *Eunuchus*, we find the soldier's parasite Gnatho.

At the beginning of Act II, scene 2 (232), Gnatho is commenting upon a man whom he just met in the street and who, like himself, had gobbled up his inheritance and was reduced to beggary — *squalidum, aegrum, pannis annisque obsitum* (236) — dirty, ill, smothered in his rags and his years. The fellow is hopeless. Why not be a parasite like Gnatho himself — the obvious solution to his problem? The man replies *at ego infelix neque ridiculus esse neque plagas pati possum* (244) — "But I, poor wretch, cannot be a funny-man or a slapstick clown." He cannot then bring himself to do what Ergasilus proclaims parasites must do (cf. *Capt*. 88-90 *nisi qui colaphos perpeti potest parasitus frangique aulas in caput* and 471 *nil morantur iam . . . plagipatidas*).

Then comes the answer "What, do you think that is how things are done? You are on the wrong track altogether" and Gnatho goes on to explain (246ff.):

> *Olim isti fuit generi quondam quaestus apud saeclum prius:*
> *hoc novomst aucupium; ego adeo hanc primus inveni viam.*

est genus hominum qui esse primos se omnium rerum volunt
nec sunt: hos consector; hisce ego non paro me ut rideant,
sed eis ultro adrideo et eorum ingenia admiror simul.
quidquid dicunt laudo; id rursum si negant, laudo id quoque;
negat quis: nego: ait: aio: postremo imperavi egomet mihi
omnia adsentari. is quaestus nunc est multo uberrimus.

At one time, in the last generation, there was a living
for that kind of person [i.e. the *parasitus ridiculus*]. This
is the new way of catching patrons; in fact I was the
first to find it. There is a class of men who want to be
first in everything and yet they are not. These I pursue,
I do not contrive that they should laugh at my jokes,
but I make it my business to smile upon them and at
the same time to admire them for their abilities.
Whatever they say I approve; if they say No to
something, that too I approve. If someone says No, I
say No; he says Yes, I say Yes. In a word I have trained
myself to agree to everything. This nowadays is much
the most profitable livelihood.

For the *ridiculi* (*isti generi*) there was a livelihood *apud*
saeclum prius. This last is a somewhat vague remark but if it
means "in the previous generation" then it brings us back to
the time of Plautus, writing some forty years before Terence
(the *Stichus* was produced in 200, the *Eunuchus* in 161 B.C.), to
Gelasimus and Ergasilus (and perhaps Peniculus?) who are
ridiculi and *plagipatidae*, who once made a living but have
ceased to do so out of their *dicta ridicula*. The new parasite, as
Gnatho tells us, must be simply a flatterer, saying Yes and
No, like Peniculus does (*Menaechmi* 162).

Gnatho, it must be remembered, is a soldier's parasite, the
only such character in Terence. He belongs to the same

category as Artotrogus of the *Miles* and Cleomachus' servant in the *Bacchides* (see above, p. 8). All three earn their keep solely by flattery (Art. *adsentandumst quidquid hic mentibitur* — *Miles* 35). Gnatho has a more active part than the other two but, like theirs, his remarks aside show his true feelings regarding his patron.

The lengthy monologue (37 lines — 232ff.), in which Gnatho is presented to us and explains his philosophy of life, reminds us forcibly of the similar monologues in which Plautus presents his leading slaves and parasites. The parasite is found in Greek comedy but is not given the importance he receives in Plautus. Terence's handling of Gnatho is a reflection of the importance given by his predecessor to the parasite role. If this is so, then the reproach made by Luscius Lanuvinus at the play's rehearsal, declaring that the roles of parasite and boastful soldier were taken from old plays by Naevius and Plautus, was probably genuine. In which case, Terence's critic was in all likelihood objecting, not to the roles of parasite and soldier as such, for the former at least must have appeared in the Greek model, Menander's *Colax* (The Flatterer), as the title implies, but to the expansion of Gnatho's role along Plautine (Naevian) lines that we have in the monologue 232ff. It is relevant to remark that we have from the lips of Gnatho a picture of Roman life in the *macellum*, similar to glimpses afforded us in the plays of Plautus. We meet the *cuppedinarii, cetarii, lanii, coqui, fartores* and *piscatores* (256-7) the delicatessen merchants, butchers, fishmongers etc., with whom he is on intimate terms and whose gossip will be welcome to his patron's ears. Gnatho has thus become an *obsonator*, performing the function which Ergasilus had complained the young masters had taken over from their parasites (*Capt*.474). In 813f. he rants against the *piscatores, lanii, pistores* etc.

I have digressed at length on Gnatho because he discusses the fate of the professional jester in Roman society, telling how he must abandon his jests for mere flattery. The *ridiculus* of the previous generation (*apud saeclum prius*) has now to be the *assentator* (*imperavi egomet mihi omnia adsentari*) in order to live. Plautus links Peniculus with the jester Ergasilus through their common introduction by the *Iuventus*, but he has no *dicta* and is already an *assentator*. We must conclude that the procedure which Gnatho advocates and declares to have invented (*Eun.*247) has already been adopted by Peniculus. On the surface this is merely a fictional situation in Roman comedy. But the fact that Plautus refers in emphatic terms to the decline of the *parasitus ridiculus* and his art in more than one play and the fact that Terence specifically recalls the situation, in a peculiarly Plautine passage in a play of alleged indebtedness to his predecessors in Roman comedy, suggests that the *ridiculus* was a real figure in Roman society. The same is true of the *Iuventus*, the anonymous Young Men, whom Ergasilus specifically blames for the decline of the jester's calling. They are not Philopolemus and his friends, nor Menaechmus and his. They are Roman and real. We shall meet them in the following chapters and endeavour to explain why they displace the jester *ridiculus* and his jest-books.

There is one more professional jester to consider. He is Saturio of the *Persa*. Toxilus, the protagonist of the play, who triumphantly conducts his love affair to the discomfiture of the pimp Dordalus, is actually a slave, indulging in a royal bout of freedom (*basilice agito eleutheria* — 28) during his master's absence abroad. He assumes the attributes of a free man and, among them, acquires the services of a parasite, Saturio.

The latter appears at the beginning of Act I, scene 2 (53)

and at once proclaims his calling to be an ancient one, in fact
hereditary —

> *Veterem atque antiquom quaestum maiorum meum*
> *servo atque obtineo et magna cum cura colo. . . .*
> *pater, avos, proavos, abavos, atavos, tritavos*
> *quasi mures semper edere alienum cibum, . . .*
> *atque eis cognomentum erat duris Capitonibus.*

The old and indeed ancient calling of my ancestors
I hold and maintain and cultivate with great care . . .;
my father, grandfather and his father and grandfather
like mice always ate other peoples' food . . ., and
indeed they were nicknamed the Hard-Headed Ones.

Immediately we recall Ergasilus, who makes the identical
remark about mice (*Capt.*77) and suggests the need for a hard
head (*nisi qui colaphos perpeti potest parasitus frangique aulas in
caput*, ibid, 88-9). Both are then *plagipatidae* — slapstick
clowns.

Saturio now launches an attack upon the class of professional informers, the *quadrupulatores*, against whom he
desires to see legislation restricting their financial profit from
delation (62-74). Plautus is aiming here to give a Roman
background to Saturio's remarks, but one is also reminded of
Gelasimus' attack (*Stich.*198f.) on the *curiosi malevoli, alienas res
qui curant* (above, p. 13) which may refer to the same people.
Incidentally, Ergasilus has his *bête noire* in the *Iuventus* who
care only for themselves (*Capt.*104) while Gnatho attacks the
genus hominum qui esse primos se omnium rerum volunt nec sunt
(*Eun.*248). Could it be that the informers, the maliciously
curious and the self-seekers are in some way to be linked as
common enemies of the professional jester? I mention the
point only because these unlikeable characteristics apply

rather significantly to the subject of our next chapter, the *scurrae* of Plautus.

In 123ff., Saturio stresses the parasite's dependent role. He must not have money of his own, otherwise he would squander it in providing for himself instead of letting others do it. He must have the minimum equipment of the itinerant Cynic beggar.

> *cynicum esse egentem oportet parasitum probe:*
> *ampullam, strigilem, scaphium, soccos, pallium,*
> *marsuppium habeat, inibi paullum praesidi,*
> *qui familiarem suam vitam oblectet modo.*

> The parasite must really be a beggar Cynic; let
> him have his flask, his blade, his cup, shoes,
> cloak and wallet, with just enough therein to
> provide for his own family comfort.

Here then are the parasite's *ornamenta*, the items characteristic of his semi-vagrant profession and with which he no doubt appeared on stage. We recall that Gelasimus also spoke of his *strigil* and flask (*Stich*.230). The reference to the beggar Cynic is not without interest; there may have been a link in tradition between the vagrant Cynic philosopher who sweetened his teaching with humorous anecdote and the professional jester whom we meet in Plautus.

Saturio, like Gelasimus, also has his jest-books. He will furnish them as a dowry for his daughter (392ff.).

> *librorum eccillum habeo plenum soracum . . .*
> *dabuntur dotis tibi inde sescenti logi,*
> *atque Attici omnes; nullum Siculum acceperis:*
> *cum hac dote poteris vel mendico nubere.*

> Here I have a hamper full of books; you shall
> have scores of jests from it for your dowry and

all of them Attic jokes, not a Sicilian among
them. With such a dowry you can marry even a
beggar,
or a beggar if you like (*vel mendico*) (and nothing more?).

The manner is typically Plautine. The Attic/Sicilian allusion
is however obscure and may or may not come from a Greek
model. Does it imply that the parasites in the early Sicilian
comedies, like those of Epicharmus (5th century B.C.) also had
jest-books and that their jokes (*dicta, logi*) were worse than
those of Athenian jesters? We may compare the remark in
Men. Prol. 11-12 *hoc argumentum graecissat, tamen non atticissat,
verum sicilicissat* — "this plot has a Greek flavour; however,
not an Attic, but a Sicilian flavour". It is certainly not from
the Greek model and is obscure, although there is an allusion
to the fact that the father of the Menaechmi twins belongs to
Syracuse.

It is to be noted that Plautus' *ridiculi*, while referring to
their *dicta*, do not actually treat us to samples of them. This is
probably because such *dicta*, as the stock in trade of the
professional jester of real life, were a professional secret and
Plautus would not be allowed to make use of such *dicta* for
the humour of his *palliatae*. Moreover, Plautus does not make
use of the *ridiculus'* special talents for the purpose of
furthering his plots. The *ridiculus* is, like his fellow parasites,
the outrageous flatterer and the resourceful intriguer, a
character whose appearance on stage incites mirth, but
Plautus' handling of Gelasimus, Ergasilus and also of
Peniculus shows a desire to pinpoint the decline of the jester's
role through their abandonment by the anonymous *Iuventus*,
the Men about Town who are their patrons.

I have been concerned in this first part of my study to
show, by means of what I believe are relevant quotations,

that the professional jester is a real figure in the contemporary world of Plautus. And yet he is not a *scurra*, the traditional jester of Roman literature throughout the ages. For the latter also has his place in the pages of Plautus, where, paradoxically, he is neither a jester nor does he play a part in the action! In other words, Plautus makes reference in his plays to *scurrae* in the same way that he refers to the *Iuventus* who are also not characters of *palliatae*.

III

The Scurra *in Plautus*

It is in the pages of Plautus that we meet the *scurra* for the first time in literature and it is at first sight a surprising encounter, for the sum total of characteristics which emerge from the playwright's remarks seem to have little relevance to the *saltator fabularum*, to the *ioculator* and to the *mimicus*, which threefold identity is traditionally the *scurra*'s in Classical and Imperial times as also indeed in the Middle Ages and beyond.

The most comprehensive description given by Plautus of the *scurra* is provided by the indignant outburst of the old man Megaronides in the *Trinummus*. He is angry with himself for having misjudged the conduct of his friend Callicles in buying Charmides' house to protect the latter's interests. The fact is that he has been misled as to his friend's character and intentions by listening to ill-informed gossip on the part of a noxious group of rumour-mongers (*Trin.*199ff.):

> *Nihil est profecto stultius neque stolidius*
> *neque mendaciloquius neque argutum magis,*
> *neque confidentiloquius neque periurius*
> *quam urbani assidui cives quos scurras vocant.*

Nothing is indeed more foolish or more stupid or more mendacious or more malicious, or more self-assured or more deceitful than those officious City wits whom people call *scurrae*.

The last line of the quotation of course raises a translation problem. The expression *urbani cives* would seem to impart a Roman flavour, lifting the line out from any context in a Greek model (the setting of the *Trinummus* is Athens) and *scurra* is a "Latin" term, whatever its dialectal origin. *Assidui* is difficult; it often means "officious", which is suitable here, but it is also an archaic term for *locuples* ("well-to-do") and Cicero speaks of *scurrae locupletes* or *divites*. Nixon (Loeb Library, Plautus Vol. V, p. 116) translates *assidui* as "busybodies", while Ernout (Budé edition, Plaute Vol. VII, p. 28) renders *Trin.*202 "ces bourgeois occupés sans cesse à battre le pavé". But Plautus does not say *assidui homines* which one would naturally translate as "officious people", but *assidui cives*. I submit that in our context *assiduus* is the word for which Cicero, Varro, Quintilian, Gellius and others give a traditional derivation from *as* and *dare*, i.e. "tribute-payer" and so "well-to-do citizen" (Fr. "bien assis"). Cf. Cic. *Rep.*2.22.40 *cum locupletes assiduos appellasset* (sc. Servius Tullius) *ab aere dando*; Gell. 16.10.15 *assiduus in XII Tabulis pro locuplete dictus*. Publius Clodius, it was alleged, offered his tender youth to the lusts of wealthy libertines, *aetatulam suam ad scurrarum locupletium libidines detulit* (Cic. *de Harus. Resp.*42) and was in fact a *locupletium scurrarum scortum* (*Sest.*39).

Megaronides continues his outburst, blaming himself for being taken in by the *falsa verba* of these fellows (205 ff.):

> *qui omnia se simulant scire neque quicquam sciunt.*
> *quod quisque in animo habet aut habiturust sciunt,*
> *sciunt id quod in aurem rex reginae dixerit,*
> *sciunt quod Iuno fabulatast cum Iove;*
> *quae neque futura neque sunt, tamen illi sciunt.*
> *falson an vero laudent, culpent quem velint,*
> *non flocci faciunt, dum illud quod lubeai sciant.*

They pretend they know everything and they don't know anything. They know what everyone has in mind or is going to have in mind. They know what the king said to the queen. They know what Juno talked about to Jupiter. The things that neither are nor will be they know all the same. They do not give a damn whether their praise or blame of whomever they will be true or false, providing they appear to know whatever takes their fancy.

We are reminded of Gelasimus' remark (*Stich.*198ff.) about the *curiosi mali*, the inquisitive, malicious types who mind other people's business, having none of their own. His fellow parasite Saturio of the *Persa* mentioned a similar class of busybodies (62-76), the professional informers or *quadrupulatores*, against whose activities he would like to see new legislation. It would seem that Plautus loses no opportunity to inveigh against a social menace of his own day. However this is not to say that the *scurrae*, whom Megaronides identifies with *urbani assidui cives*, are also inevitably *quadrupulatores*, although one imagines that delation is occasionally an indulgence of theirs.

Megaronides' *scurra* is then a know-all, privy to everyone's secrets and heedless of the justification of his praise or blame. Hence, his praise is not worth having, and so Stratophanes, the boastful soldier of the *Truculentus*, informs us (491) *non placet quem scurrae laudant*, implying that his own exploits bear the proof of actual witness — *qui audiunt audita dicunt, qui vident plane sciunt* (490) — "Those who actually hear tell what they have heard, those who see plainly know."

But it appears that *scurrae* are not only purveyors of scandal, but are also given to making fun of people. The soldier Antamonides in *Poen.* 1280 says *si ego minam non ultus*

*fuero probe, quam lenoni dedi, tum profecto me sibi habento scurrae
ludificatui* — "if I do not properly take revenge for the cash I
gave to the pimp, then indeed let the *scurrae* have me for their
sport". This remark is surely significant, for it implies not
only that the *scurra* has a jesting, satirical turn of humour, but
also that he is something of a social institution, recognized
not only for his scandal-mongering but also for this jesting
quality.

Now there can be no doubt that the scene in which
Antamonides appears (*Poen.*V.5) is for the most part Plautine
invention, not part of his Greek model, for it contains the
usual dosage of Roman allusions which we find in these
innovations, e.g. *tune hic amator audes esse . . . plenior ali ulpicique
quam Romani remiges?* — "you dare to play the lover here . . .
though fuller of garlic and leek than a team of Roman
oarsmen?" (*Poen.*1310f.). It resembles in this the extra-
numerary scenes in which Plautus develops his *parasiti
ridiculi*.

Megaronides' outburst is no less an interpolation, intro-
ducing the *scurrae* who are as Roman as the *parasiti ridiculi*. It
comes right at the end of the first act of the *Trinummus*, after
he has dismissed Callicles and he is left alone with his
thoughts. We may note also that both Stratophanes of the
Truculentus and Antamonides of the *Poenulus* are boastful
soldiers, a type particularly dear to Plautus who lards their
conversation with military expressions suited to the taste of
his Roman audience. Stratophanes' tirade against the *scurrae*
is addressed to the audience and he speaks of "those whose
tongue sharpens the edge of a domestic sword" (*illi quorum
lingua gladiorum aciem praestringit domi* — 492). He has no use
for the *civis argutus* (an echo of Megaronides' *nihil argutum
magis*) and his remark *sine virtute argutum civem mihi habeam pro
praefica, quae alios conlaudat, eapse sese vero non potest* (495-6) —

"a City-wit without manly virtue I would rate no higher than
a hired woman mourner who praises others but cannot praise
herself" besides containing a specifically Roman allusion (the
praefica) reminds us of the stage-manager (*choragus* — another
Plautine interpolation), who in the first scene of Act IV of the
Curculio speaks of the malicious gossips who gather at the
water-tank outside the City-walls — *confidentes garrulique et
malevoli supera lacum, qui alteri de nihilo audacter dicunt con-
tumeliam et qui ipsi sat habent quod in se possit vere dicier* (477-479)
— "the self-assured, gossipy, malicious types about the
water-tank, who boldly make insulting remarks à propos of
nothing against some other person and who have quite
enough that can truthfully be told against themselves".

How similar is this observation to that made by Gelasimus
the *parasitus ridiculus* at *Stich.* 198ff.: *sed curiosi sunt hic complures
mali, alienas res qui curant studio maximo, quibus ipsis nullast res,
quam procurent, sua* (noted in section II p. 13). He adds, *i quando
quem auctionem facturum sciunt, adeunt, perquirunt quid siet causae
ilico, alienum aes cogat an pararit praedium, uxorin sit reddenda dos
divortio* — "these people know when someone is about to
hold an auction, they attend and enquire as to the reason for it
— is he compelled by debt or has he bought an estate, or must
he pay back the wife's dowry in a divorce case?" Are these
curiosi not like the *urbani assidui cives* of Megaronides and the
quadrupulatores of Saturio, whose ranks he refuses to join? —
*neque enim decet sine meo periclo ire alienum ereptum bona neque illi
qui faciunt mihi placent* (*Persa* 62-64) — "it is not right to
proceed to rob other folk of their property, without risk to
oneself (i.e. as an informer) and I don't like those who do
this".

These interesting parallels lead one to deduce that Plautus
is linking the people of whom his *parasiti riduculi*, Gelasimus,
Ergasilus, Saturio and Peniculus, complain, namely the ex-

patrons who reject these entertainers, with the people of whom Megaronides, Antamonides, Stratophanes and the Choragus complain. The former category would seem to be collectively referred to as the *Iuventus*, the Young Men of Rome; the latter are described by Megaronides as *urbani assidui cives quos scurras vocant*. It is tempting to regard both groups as one and the same, especially when we consider the similar technique of presentation. Ergasilus of the *Captivi* is presented at the beginning of Act I, in a long monologue, introduced by the significant word *Iuventus (nomen indidit Scorto mihi)*. Peniculus of the *Menaechmi* is presented at the beginning of Act I in a long monologue opening with *Iuventus (nomen fecit Peniculo mihi)*. Gelasimus of the *Stichus* also first appears in a long monologue beginning Act I, scene 3. Saturio of the *Persa* is introduced in a long monologue beginning Act I, scene 2.

Similarly, Megaronides of the *Trinummus* indulges his tirade against the *scurrae* in a monologue of twenty-four lines, devoted entirely to the subject, at the end of Act I. Antamonides has a long grumble to himself at the beginning of Act V of the *Poenulus* and Stratophanes' boastings and complaints are addressed to the spectators for fifteen lines at the beginning of Act II, scene 6 of the *Truculentus*. The Choragus inserts his remarks on the *confidentes garrulique et malevoli supera lacum* amid a host of other Roman allusions (the shrine of Cloacina, the temple of Castor, the vicus Tuscus, the Velabrum) in a monologue of twenty-five lines at the beginning of Act IV of the *Curculio*.

Thus, in each case where the selfish young men and the malicious busybodies are discussed, the action of the play is suspended by amplifications which bear the stamp of Plautus' exuberant spirit and are full of abusive language and reminiscent of the Roman scene. One is left with the impression that

Plautus himself is personally concerned to draw the attention of his audience to a class of person who belong to the real world of his own day and who, in fact, are a social menace.

Collybiscus, the bailiff in the *Poenulus*, à propos of the remark of the advocates *nos priores ibimus* (611) observes *faciunt scurrae quod consuerunt, pone sese homines locant* — "they do what the *scurrae* are in the habit of doing, they put themselves in front of people". We are reminded of the selfish behaviour of the *Iuventus* in the *Captivi*, where Ergasilus remarks (477) *neque ridiculos iam terrunci faciunt, sese omnes amant* — "they don't give a brass farthing for the funny-men, they are in love with themselves alone", echoing his previous words at 104 *nulla est spes iuventutis, sese omnes amant*.

Still more are we reminded of Gnatho's words at Ter. *Eun.*248 — *est genus hominum qui esse primos se omnium rerum volunt nec sunt* — "there is a race of men who want to be first in everything and yet they are not". Gnatho is a soldier's parasite retainer, who has learnt by experience not to be a funny-man scapegoat, and has turned mere flatterer and yes-man to the same kind of selfish patrons as those at whose hands Gelasimus and company suffer rejection, in other words the *Iuventus*.

The prime significance of this remark of Gnatho's is not that it confirms the other remarks we have noted about selfish patrons, but that it is uttered by a character in Terence. Gnatho and his master, the boastful soldier Thraso, are the only such pair of characters in Terence and Gnatho alone in Terence discusses the lot of the *parasitus ridiculus* in his advice to Parmeno who cannot bring himself to be one — *at ego infelix neque ridiculus esse neque plagas pati possum* (244). There seems to be little doubt that Terence adopted the soldier and his parasite roles from Plautus, in spite of his denial in the Prologue (25-26). If he did, he is echoing a Roman situation outlined by Plautus; if he did not, he is still echoing a Roman situation, the decline of the *ridiculus* as an entertainer, which situation he significantly describes as belonging to a previous generation — *apud saeclum prius* (246) i.e. the time of Plautus. It is also significant that Luscius, who was present at a rehearsal of the *Eunuchus* in 161 B.C., referred in his charge of plagiarism only to the fact that the roles of parasite and soldier were taken from Plautus (and Naevius). This would seem to clinch the matter; Terence had adopted the two roles and the situation described by Gnatho from Roman versions of Menander's *Flatterer* and the implication is that the soldier and parasite team were not to be found in Menander, but only in the versions of Plautus and/or Naevius.

I believe then that we may link together the selfish *Iuventus* patrons of the *ridiculi* and the malicious gossiping *scurrae* and that they constitute a purely Roman phenomenon.

We saw from Antamonides' remark quoted above, from *Poen.*1280, that *scurrae* indulge in mockery (*ludificatus*), which is something we might expect of the arrogant, malicious gossips the other references reveal. Nevertheless, it is a new aspect and one more in keeping with the *scurra* of later tradition, who is of course a jester. At the same time, this conduct is in keeping with the jesting spirit shown by the *Iuventus* in bestowing comic names upon their parasites (*Capt.*69, *Men.*77 — Scortum and Peniculus). Indeed Ergasilus remarks (71) *scio absurde dictum hoc derisores dicere* "I know they say this absurdity in the spirit of mockery".

Confirmation of this playful spirit comes from Curculio, who, in a typically Plautine passage, is acting the *servus currens* type of role, knocking all the street loungers out of his way, in his hurry to meet up with Phaedromus. Among the people who must get out of his way are *isti qui ludunt datatim servi scurrarum in via, et datores et factores omnis subdam sub solum* —

"those servants of the *scurrae* who play ball games in the street — the bowlers and the batsmen I will knock them all into the ground" (*Curc.*296-7). The implication is that the servants behave like their masters, indulging in light-hearted irresponsible behaviour in the streets. They show as little regard for people's comfort as for their reputations! On the *scurra* as ball-player (juggler?) cf. Lucilius, *Satiren*, ed. W. Krenkel, Leiden, Brill, 1970 frg.1150: *Coelius collusor Galloni scurra trigonum cum ludit* — "The *scurra* Coelius when he plays ball with Gallonius . . ."

Act I of the *Mostellaria* opens with the comic pair, Tranio the Town slave and Grumio, his counterpart from the master's country estate. Tranio plies Grumio with abuse, blows and witticism, so that Grumio retorts *tu urbanus vero scurra, deliciae popli, rus mihi tu obiectas?* (15-16) — "you City wit [jester?, clown?], you idol of the crowd, do you throw my country ways in my face?" Tranio then would seem to be a *servus scurrae*, like those referred to by Curculio. We know from Megaronides that the *scurrae* are *urbani*, but Grumio goes on to berate Tranio for his conduct in corrupting the younger master — *dum tibi lubet, licetque, pota, perde rem, corrumpe erilem adulescentem optumum; dies noctesque bibite, pergraecamini, amicas emite liberate, pascite parasitos, obsonate pollucibiliter* (20-4) — "while you want and while you can, go on drinking, wasting the estate, corrupting our excellent young master; drink by day and by night, thoroughly play the Greek, buy girl-friends and set them free, feed the parasites and do your shopping on the grand scale".

The *scurrae* and their servants emerge from this tirade as Young Men About Town, given to extravagant living and debauchery. The jibe *obsonate* reminds us of Ergasilus' complaint against the *Iuventus* — *ipsi obsonant, quae parasitorum ante erat provincia* (*Capt.*474) — "they themselves do the shopping which used to be the parasites' responsibility".

Urbanus scurra, deliciae popli, rus mihi tu obiectas? — here is something rather different from the attributes Plautus has elsewhere listed for us, although we saw from Antamonides' remark (*Poen.*1280) that the *scurrae* are sometimes *ludificatores*. Grumio is a country clown, Tranio a City wit — a classic comic pair. For the first time one senses here a theatrical connotation for the *scurra*. The phrase *deliciae popli* suggests a favourite entertainer, a figure from popular humorous tradition. Does he belong to mime or to the Atellan farce? Cicero informs us (see section I, p. 4) that *scurra* is a Latin word and presumably he is an Italian, not a Greek institution. If then the *scurra* belongs to the Roman stage, what of the *urbani assidui cives quos scurras vocant*? (Megaronides). They belong to the City (*urbani*), they are free-born citizens (*cives*) and possibly well-to-do (*assidui*). They cannot be professional artistes. They must therefore be amateurs. Eduard Fraenkel discusses the Plautine critical character-sketches such as *Trin.*199ff. and *Bacch.*1087ff. in his *Elementi Plautini*, pp. 177ff. The procedure may well hark back to Old and New Comedy, but the subject-matter is surely Roman.

There is another reference to the *scurra* in Plautus which we must link with *Mostellaria* 15, because it is uttered by a Country slave to the equivalent of a Town slave in a similar scene of comic repartee. This time the pair are Epidicus and Thesprio, who appear in the first scene of the *Epidicus*, as Tranio and Grumio appear in the first scene of *Mostellaria*. Tranio and Grumio are both slaves of the prodigal youth Philolaches; Epidicus and Thesprio both serve the young Stratippocles, who has been on active service abroad and is now returning home. Epidicus as a servant of the Town house has stayed at home, but Thesprio had accompanied his master in the campaigning. As Thesprio is hastening homewards from the harbour with vigorous strides, Epidicus accosts him but has difficulty in keeping pace. He reproaches Thesprio, who replies (*Epid.*15) *scurra es*, to which Epidicus answers *scio te esse equidem hominem militarem*. These remarks presumably mean "You are a Townie" i.e. out of condition, "Of course I know you are a military man" i.e. fighting fit. Compare the use of the term *scurra* for a Praetorian Guardsman in later times, because the Guards, while garrisoned in Town as the Emperor's bodyguard, lost their fighting fitness and became "soft", e.g. *Hist.Aug.: Vita Sev.Alex.*61 *unus ex Germanis, qui scurrarum* [= *praetorianorum*] *officium sustinebat*; *Elagab.*33.7 *occisus est per scurras* — "he was murdered by Guardsmen".

We are bound to consider the *Mostellaria* and the *Epidicus* references together, since they occur in similar contexts. Thesprio refers merely to the *scurra*'s "softness", while Grumio mentions not only his debauched way of life but also his City wit and his popularity with the crowd. But Thesprio's remark does indicate that the significance of the professional *scurra*'s role in mime must have been that he was the Townie, as opposed to the country clown. Thus Tranio and Epidicus are themselves *scurrae* in essence or, perhaps preferably *servi scurrarum*, and the fact that Plautus does not describe them as such is evidence that the *scurra* is not part of the *palliata* tradition. The *scurra* in any case belongs to mime and it may be that his role therein is that of smart City wastrel and/or his slave (the *servus scurrae*). Tranio and Epidicus as Town slaves, sharp-witted and soft living, play roles similar to that which must have been the role of the professional stage *scurra*, in which then his art as *saltator* and *ioculator* consisted.

Why should Megaronides' *urbani assidui cives* be called *scurrae* by the general public who have to suffer from their conduct? The implication of Megaronides' remarks is that it is because they are stupid, mendacious, arrogant and deceitful; they know everyone's secrets and they are malicious gossips, distributing praise and blame in arbitrary fashion. Antamonides adds that they make fun of people. The stage-manager in *Curculio* and Gelasimus in the *Stichus* refer to the same kind of people. Collybiscus tells us that they are self-assertive, reminding us of the similar selfish conduct of the *Iuventus* as described by Ergasilus. Like master, like man, and Tranio, who is a *servus scurrae*, aids and abets his young master in his feasting and debauchery, behaving irresponsibly as do the *servi scurrarum in via* as described by Curculio. They go on shopping sprees and visit the brothels as do the *Iuventus* in the *Captivi* — *ipsi obsonant, quae parasitorum ante erat provincia, ipsi de foro tam aperto capite ad lenones eunt ...* (475-6).

The answer must be that the conduct of these Young Men About Town reflects that of the professional stage character — the *scurra mimicus*, as he is called throughout the centuries, though not in Plautus, whose sole reference to the professional player would seem to be the phrase *deliciae popli* (*Most.*15). The colloquial spelling *popli* suggests that the phrase is a cliché — "Top of the Pops", and cf. *Asin.*655 *decus popli*.

The professional *scurra*'s role in mime must then be that of a malicious, witty, gossiping, interfering, arrogant nuisance. Megaronides' amateurs are *urbani*; Tranio the Townie is also an *urbanus scurra*, and the *scurra* is often described in later times too as *urbanus* and as *dicax* (witty and malicious), which attribute accords perfectly with Quintilian's definition of *dicacitas* as *sermonem cum risu aliquos incessentem* — "language attacking individuals with ridicule" (6.3.21). To be *urbanus* implies a sharpened City wit as opposed to the slowness of the *rusticus*, and the impudent slave Truculentus remarks (682) *iam postquam in urbem crebro commeo, dicax sum factus, iam sum cavillator probus* — "since I have taken to coming into Town, I have become sharp-witted. I am now a proper jester." The *cavillatio*, the jesting quip, play on words, hair-splitting sophistry etc. was part of the stock in trade of all jesters and the *parasitus ridiculus* Gelasimus boasts of the *cavillationes, adsentatiunculas ac perieratiunculas parasiticas* — "jestings, little flatteries and deceits" of his *logi* or jest-books (*Stich*.228-9).

I have boldly equated the *urbani assidui cives/scurrae* of Megaronides with the selfish ex-patrons of Gelasimus and company, the *Iuventus* — the Young Men About Town — and declare the Town to be the Rome of Plautus' day. The question now arises as to why should the *Iuventus* reject the services of the *parasiti ridiculi*, the professional funny-men, whom they used to employ?

Superficially, the answer is provided by Ergasilus' *ipsi obsonant* — the Young Men have taken upon themselves the parasites' role and, as Ergasilus twice remarks in six lines, they have done so deliberately, have agreed among themselves not to laugh at the funny-men's jokes — *dico unum ridiculum dictum de dictis melioribus . . . nemo ridet; scivi extemplo rem de compecto geri; pergo ad alios, venio ad alios, deinde ad alios: una res! omnes de compecto rem agunt, quasi in Velabro olearii* — "I tell one of my jests from the best of my repertory . . . no one laughs; at once I know it's a put-up job. I go from one lot to the other — it's all the same! They are all acting in concert, like the oil-men in the Velabrum" (*Capt*.482-9).

If the Young Men are dispensing with the services and with the jests of the *ridiculi*, is it because they are taking it upon themselves to provide for themselves, not only the shopping and the gossip to be learned at market and water-

tank, but also the *ridicularia* of their former entertainers?
Certainly, if the amateur *scurrae* are to live up to the role of
their professional counterparts, they must be constant prac-
titioners of *iocularia*. If then we are right in equating the
Iuventus derisores with the amateur *scurrae*, then we must
assume that these former patrons have dispensed with
the jests of their *parasiti ridiculi* in order to practise their
own.

But why should they do this? Was there not room in the
Roman world of the leisured Young Man for two kinds of
humorous expression — assuming that there was a distinction between the *ridicularia* of Gelasimus and company and
the *iocularia* of the amateur and professional *scurrae*? It would
seem from the complaints of the *ridiculi* that there was not
room for both. How could this be?

All this is speculation, to which a positive answer cannot
be forthcoming. But we have the undoubted fact of the clash
between the *Iuventus* and the *parasitus ridiculus*. Could it be a
question of a conflict of traditions? Do the *ridiculi* represent
one school of humorous technique and the amateur *scurrae*
another?

We have seen in section II that the *ridiculi* of Plautus pursue
an hereditary vocation and are professionals, possessing a
repertory of jest-books (*dicta, logi*). If there is a humorous
tradition behind them it would appear to be that of the
vagrant beggar philosopher Cynics, the followers of
Diogenes of Sinope (c.400-c.325 B.C.). They renounced all
worldly possessions and pursued a life of poverty, based
merely on the satisfying of Man's basic, natural needs,
practising asceticism and defying convention. Their flagrant
denunciation of self-seeking careerism and socially advan-
tageous virtues earned them a reputation for shamelessness, a
behaviour no more edifying than that of dogs — hence the

nickname (κύων) bestowed upon the founder of the movement. Certain notables among the Cynics, like Menippus of Gadara (first half of the 3rd century B.C.), evolved a kind of humour in their satirical treatment of philosophical themes — the serio-comic style (σπουδογέλοιον) as it came to be called.

The Cynic philosopher led a vagrant life and equipped himself with a traveller's needs, a cloak and staff, a wallet, flask, knife and cup. If invited to a meal, he would content himself with the humblest place at the lowest bench.

Now, curiously enough, all this is reflected in the remarks of Plautus' *parasiti ridiculi*. We saw in section II (p. 24) that Saturio (*Persa*123ff.) refers to the items of equipment when he declares that the parasite must indeed be a beggar Cynic (*cynicum esse egentem oportet parasitum probe*). Gelasimus too refers to his *strigil* and flask (*Stich*.230). These items must have formed part of the *ornamenta* with which the *ridiculus* appeared on stage in Plautus' plays and which thus identified him to the audience. This itself implies that there was a traditional garb for this role. Furthermore, when Gelasimus is scrounging an invitation to dinner from Epignomus, he remarks "I do not ask to recline on a couch; you know I am a man of the lowest bench" (*hau postulo med in lecto accumbere: scis tu me esse imi subselli virum* — *Stich*.488-9). Ergasilus claims this same humble status when he complains that the Young Men care nothing for "the Spartans of the lowest bench, they who get slapped" (*nil morantur iam Lacones imi subselli viros, plagipatidas* — *Capt*.471). Stichus, the slave protagonist, also remarks on the Cynics' humble status — "We are being entertained here upon benches in the Cynic fashion rather than upon couches" (*potius in subselliis cynice hic accipimur quam in lectis* — *Stich*.704).

All this confirms the idea that the *parasitus ridiculus* is somehow associated in his way of life, that of the vagrant dependent with a gift of humorous expression, with the Cynic who likewise resorts to jesting in his diatribes against the Establishment.

It is a well-known trait of the Cynic movement that it had a special veneration for Herakles, the hero of magnificent labours, the warrior liberator, benefactor of Mankind. In lighter mood, the Cynic literary genre known as Menippean satire parodies its hero, making him out to be a misused general factotum of the gods, an errand boy and dogsbody. He is so represented in the satire, ascribed to Seneca the Philosopher, called the *Ludus de Morte Claudii*. It is worth noting therefore that at least one of Plautus' *ridiculi* refers to Hercules as his patron. Gelasimus (*Stich.*218ff.) declares that he must sell off his stock of jokes and his rusty knife and flask that he may pay off a ten per cent due to Hercules — *uti decumam partem Herculi polluceam* (233). At 386 his fortunes have changed and he will no longer sell; Hercules will get an increased offering — *Hercules, decumam esse adauctam quam vovi gratulor*. Discomfited again by 395, he changes his mind and decides again to sell, reproaching the god for his poor showing as a patron — *Hercules, qui deus sis, sane discessisti non bene* — "Hercules, although you are a god, you have come off badly in this affair."

Thus it is not impossible that the professional funny men of Plautus hark back to a comic tradition associated with their vagrant counterparts, the Cynic beggar philosophers, and that they also claim Hercules as their divine patron.

But what of the amateur *scurrae* whom we also meet in Plautus? If they associate themselves, through their professional counterparts, with a tradition, it must be a theatrical one, for the *scurra* is, throughout his history, a *saltator* and *ioculator*, belonging, at least originally, to mime. How are the Young Men About Town, the *Iuventus* of Plautus, the erstwhile patrons of the *ridiculi* among whom we have placed the amateur *scurrae*, involved in a theatrical tradition?

IV

The Iuventus *of Livy and the* Scurrae *of Cicero and Horace*

In section II we saw that the parasites of Plautus' plays fall into different categories. One of these categories comprises four parasites who are professional jesters — *parasiti ridiculi*. They form part of the Roman background of Plautus' own day and, while they have only minor roles in the action of the plays in which they appear, they are too developed by Plautus to be mere adoptions from a New Comedy model, although of course Greece also had its professional funny-men parasites.

Plautus also mentions in certain of his plays the *scurra*, whom we know to have been in his professional capacity a jester, a *saltator* and *ioculator* of mime. He too is a non-Greek phenomenon, for *scurra* is not a Greek term but a Roman one. But the *scurra* as described by Plautus is not a professional but an amateur, a Young Man About Town, a busybody and a malicious gossip. However, the fact that he is called *scurra* must mean that this amateur, this *iuvenis urbanus*, this *assiduus civis* as Megaronides calls him, apes the professional.

He must then be, in his malicious gossipy way, a *ioculator*. Hence the temptation, from a reading of Plautus, to link him with the jesting *Iuventus*, the patrons of the *parasiti ridiculi*, who turn aside from the latter and cease to patronize them, as the *ridiculi* complain. Incidentally, this indicates that the *parasiti ridiculi* are not themselves *scurrae* and, in fact, *scurrae* do not play a part in Plautus' plays and are not among the stock characters of *palliatae*.

That the *Iuventus* of Plautus occasionally indulge in *iocularia* is shown by the humorous appellations applied by them to Peniculus and Ergasilus (*Men.* 77-78 and *Capt.* 69-70). This penchant links them with the *Iuventus* of Livy in his account in Book 7 of their theatrical preoccupations, for they too are *ioculatores* in an amateur capacity.

Let us translate Livy's remarks and examine their significance. He is speaking of the origins of dramatic performances at Rome (7.2):

"In both this year and the one following (365-364 B.C.), during the consulship of Gaius Sulpicius Peticus and Gaius Licinius Stolo, there was a plague. In consequence, nothing worthy of historical record occurred except that for the third time since the founding of the City a ritual banquet for the gods was held to enlist their favour. Since the violence of the malady was not relieved either by human devising or by assistance from the gods, people's minds were overcome by superstition and, among other attempts at appeasement of divine wrath, it is said that a stage entertainment, a new thing for a warlike people to adopt, for earlier there had been only Circus entertainments, was instituted.

"However, it was a small thing in itself, as almost all beginnings are, and a foreign importation at that. Performers brought in from Etruria danced to the music of a flute-player, but without singing and without miming any song-material calling for imitative gesture. They provided quite graceful movements in the Etruscan fashion. The Young Men of Rome thereupon proceeded to imitate them, at the same time pouring forth jests among themselves in improvised verses, with gestures appropriate to the vocal efforts. And so the thing became accepted and by frequent practice developed.

"Meanwhile, to the native Roman performers the name *histriones* was given, since the word for player in Etruscan was *ister*. These players did not, as formerly, utter rough, improvised verses similar to the Fescennines [i.e. *rustica opprobria* — the comic abuse of country festivals] but instead performed episodic sketches complete with music and with singing adapted from now on to a flute-player and with appropriate gestures.

"Some years later Livius [Andronicus], he who first ventured to depart from the episodic sketches and to put together a play with a continuous plot and who, like all playwrights at the time, delivered his own songs, is said, when he had damaged his voice through giving repeated encores, to have obtained permission to instal a boy in front of the flautist to do the singing. Meanwhile, he himself enacted the song-material, with gestures all the more vigorous, since he was not impeded by having to use his voice.

"From then on the professional artistes began to make use of this rendering of *cantica* by mimetic gesture, the delivery of spoken passages of dialogue alone being left to their own voices. After, according to this practice, the subject-matter of drama began to be removed from the realm of laughter and uncontrolled jesting and this playful entertainment had gradually turned into an art, the Young Men abandoned the performance of plays to the professionals and themselves began to bandy jests woven into verse form according to the ancient fashion [i.e. the Fescennine tradition]. These jestings were later called *exodia* [exit-pieces or finales, probably comic sketches] and were combined for the most part with Atellan plays. This kind of entertainment was taken over from the Oscans and held on to by the Young Men, nor did they allow it to be polluted by professional players. And so the practice remains in force, that actors of Atellan plays are not removed from the tribal lists and are available for military service as having no connection with the professional theatre."

From this account of the origins of Roman drama it is clear that the *Iuventus*, the Young Men of Rome, took an interest and an active part in its development. Livy uses the collective term *Iuventus*, rather than, say, simply *iuvenes urbani*, and the fact has been taken to imply that he wished to stress that the Young Men constituted a particular class of Roman society. This view has been expounded in an important article by J. P. Morel, "La *Iuventus* et les Origines du Théâtre Romain", *Revue des Etudes Latines* 47 (1970), pp. 208-52, in which he maintains that the *Iuventus*, because they were the men of military age and therefore the most important single group in a vigorously expanding society frequently engaged in war, constituted an élite capable of imposing their ideas upon the rest of the citizen body and enjoying certain privileges and freedom of action. The view certainly commends itself and is in accordance, as Morel tells us, with a certain deference shown by Livy to the *Iuventus* in his work as a whole. Their privileged status would enable these young men to vindicate their *iocularia* as sacrosanct, having religious significance originating in fertility rites. There can be little doubt that the status given to Atellan drama was due to the insertion into it of these *iocularia* in the form of *exodia* (Livy 7.2.11), probably even performed by the young men in an amateur capacity. Hence their insistence that work of ritual significance should not be "polluted" by professionals. It is to be noted that Valerius Maximus, an historian of the reign of Tiberius, who also gives an account of the origins of Roman drama, similar in details to that of Livy, also uses the collective term *Iuventus*. His account may of course derive directly from Livy and ultimately, no doubt, from Varro.

It is also worth noting that the year 240 B.C., which is

traditionally that which witnessed the initiative of Livius Andronicus in presenting fully-fledged plays with a plot to Roman audiences, is the year following the termination of the First Punic War (264-241 B.C.). This would mean that many of the *Iuventus* would be released from military service for the time and would swell the numbers of this influential group within the City and would be free to indulge in pursuits of leisure. Many would have acquired a taste for dramatic entertainment during their service in those areas, say of Southern Italy (*Magna Graecia*), where they could become acquainted with the highly perfected Greek theatre. Hence there would be a ready-made audience in Rome itself for Andronicus and others who were to follow him, including his younger contemporary Plautus.

Andronicus was brought to Rome as a slave from his native city of Tarentum after its capture by the Romans in 272 B.C. He died about 204 B.C. and so was probably a mere boy of ten or twelve years old when captured. If we allot him a generous span of life, he was probably born about 284 B.C. After some years he passed into the service of one Lucius Livius who eventually freed him, so that he adopted, as was customary, the names of his former master and became L. Livius Andronicus. His *cognomen* tells us that he was by birth a Greek and Tarentum was largely peopled by descendants of Greek settlers. He earned a living by teaching literature and, doubtless for the benefit of his pupils, translated or para-phrased Homer's *Odyssey* into Latin. Discovering a literary bent, he proceeded to write a number of tragedies and comedies. Making a reputation at this, he was invited to present for the stage at the Ludi Romani of 240 B.C., which were held in honour of the victory ending the First Punic War, the first Latin tragedy and the first Latin comedy, adapted from Greek models.

It was perhaps about this very time that Plautus, also as a young boy, arrived at Rome from his birthplace in Umbria. He was born at Sarsina about 255 B.C. Like Andronicus, he was interested in the stage. Eventually he, like Andronicus, took to writing *fabulae palliatae*, Latin plays in Greek dress, based on Greek models. Perhaps he began, also like Andronicus, by writing impromptu sketches and translations in the Latin language in which he must early have achieved complete mastery. Andronicus' real success began in 240, so he may have begun to write some fifteen years previously, about 255, say at the age of nearly thirty. Plautus' fully-fledged *Miles Gloriosus* was written about 205. If we suppose an apprenticeship in stagecraft of some twenty years prior to the *Miles*, then Plautus could have begun to write about 225, also, by analogy with Andronicus, at about the age of thirty. If the names Maccius (from Maccus, the Atellan clown?) and Plautus ("flat-foot" of the unshod mime-player?), traditionally his, are anything to go by, he may have begun his dramatist's career by writing mimes and Atellan farces before graduating to *palliatae*. There is also much to recall the primitive episodic sketch (*satura*) in Plautus, as in the 'plotless' *Stichus* or in the flimsily linked revelry scenes of Act I of *Mostellaria*. It is tempting to speculate whether Plautus was not "warned off" composing in the manner of the farcical Atellan by the *Iuventus* of his day as being a professional *artifex artis ludicrae* and thus compelled as it were to turn to the composition of *palliatae*. This would explain his obvious antipathy to the *Iuventus* and to the amateur *scurra*.

There is no precise chronology in all this, but one thing is certain — the careers of Andronicus and of Plautus overlap, if only marginally.

Now Livy tells us that the Young Men of Rome in the

fourth century B.C. began to indulge in *iocularia* as a result of the initiative of bringing the Etruscan dancers to Rome and that these *iocularia* became a vogue and an accepted practice — *accepta itaque res saepiusque usurpando excitata* (Livy 7.2.6). So much so that, a century later, after plays with a plot had become established and handed over to professional actors (*histriones*), the Young Men, still an influential élite in Roman society, revived the *iocularia* — *more antiquo ridicula intexta versibus iactitare coepit* (sc. *Iuventus*).

This revival, if indeed it was a revival and had not remained a continuous practice, as Livy's earlier remark suggests, brings us to the time of Plautus. Indeed, the active role of the Young Men in influencing the development of the Theatre continued, for they subsequently embodied their *iocularia* into *exodia*, literally "exit-pieces" or finales which they inserted into the Atellan plays. They maintained control over this particular genre, adopted from the Oscans, and preserved it, in Livy's words, from 'pollution' by professionals, reserving for its exponents an amateur status so that they did not lose their citizen status and were entitled to perform military service. One is indeed tempted to assume from this that the Young Men themselves took part in the performance of Atellans, at least in the delivery of *exodia* containing their *ridicula intexta versibus*. Moreover, Livy informs us that this amateur status for Atellan players was continued into his own day — "and so the institution remains, that the actors of Atellans are not removed from the tribal lists and do military service, as being non-professional artists" (*expertes artis ludicrae* — 7.2.12).

Thus we are entitled to compare the *Iuventus* of whom Livy speaks with the *Iuventus* whom Plautus mentions at the beginning of Act I of the *Captivi* and of the *Menaechmi*, and, as we have seen in section III, they are indulging in *iocularia* on

both occasions, in bestowing comic nicknames upon Ergasilus and Peniculus.

Are we not then also entitled to suppose that the amateur
scurra who must also indulge in *iocularia*, since this is the
function of the professional *scurra* of mime, whom the
amateur must ape in order to merit his nickname, is to be
found in the ranks of the theatrically minded *Iuventus*? This is
my contention, and I find confirmation in Horace's description of the development of rustic merriment at harvest time
into something more sinister. Thus, from *Ep*.2.1.139-50:

> *Agricolae prisci, fortes parvoque beati,*
> *condita post frumenta levantes tempore festo*
> *corpus et ipsum animum spe finis dura ferentem* . . .
> *Tellurem porco, Silvanum lacte piabant,* . . .
> *Fescennina per hunc inventa licentia morem*
> *versibus alternis opprobria rustica fudit,*
> *libertasque recurrentis accepta per annos*
> *lusit amabiliter, donec iam saevus apertam*
> *in rabiem coepit verti iocus et per honestas*
> *ire domos impune minax.*

The old-time farmers, hardy folk and content with
little, at festival celebrations, after the corn was
gathered in, relaxing their bodies and their spirits too,
which had endured hard things in the hope of
outcome, . . . made offering of a pig to Mother Earth
and a suckling lamb to the Woodland God.

The Fescennine freedom of speech discovered in
this way poured forth rustic abuse in alternating verses
[jest and response]. This licence, becoming an accepted
form through the running years, thus continued its
amiable playfulness, until the jesting became cruel and

turned into an open savagery and pursued its way with a threatening impunity into the very homes of decent citizens.

The *saevus iocus*, the cruel jest, was the hallmark of the *scurra* in his heyday, and surely Horace, who has bitter things to say of him, as we shall see, is here referring to this social menace. He links him in the lines above with the *iocularia* derived in more innocent times from the Fescennine merriment of which Livy speaks in 7.2, and it is interesting to compare Horace's *libertas . . . accepta* with Livy's *accepta itaque res saepiusque usurpando excitata*.

The Young Men of Rome, in continuing the practice of the Etruscan *saltatio*, themselves became *saltatores*. In adding their own *iocularia* to the entertainment, they became *ioculatores* also. Now it is precisely in the double function of *saltator/ioculator* that the *scurra mimicus*, the professional, is known throughout his history. Thus the identification of the amateur *scurra* with the Young Men amateur *saltatores/ioculatores* is logical.

The *saltatio* was a rustic importation from Etruria to Rome; the *ioculatio* had its traditional origin in the rustic Fescennine merriment, also an importation from Etruria to Rome, for Fescennium was a town in Etruria. What the Roman youth did therefore was to urbanize these two forms of entertainment, hence the stock epithet of *urbanus* applied to the *scurra* (Grumio's *tu urbanus vero scurra, deliciae popli, rus mihi tu obiectas? — Most.*15). The *scurra urbanus* was established at Rome when the *rustica opprobria* became *urbana*.

As regards the *scurra mimicus* it must be mentioned here that the medieval Church Councils, in their denunciation of the theatrical world, as we shall see in section V, habitually link the terms *mimi scurraeque*. This at once denotes the link but also implies that there are two types of entertainer and that they are not one and the same.

We know for certain that the *scurra* performed in the Roman mime, even when the latter had developed from the mere episodic sketch, depicting the antics of man or beast, to a fully-fledged play with a plot, a definite literary genre, at the hands of people like Decimus Laberius and Publilius Syrus in the first century B.C. Juvenal informs us that a *scurra* played the part of a *servus fugitivus* in a mime written by one Catullus, of Nero's time — *Sat*.13, 110-111 *mimum agit ille,/urbani qualem fugitivus scurra Catulli* — "He performs a mime, such as that by witty Catullus, in which the *scurra* plays the role of a runaway slave" (and see *ad loc.* J. E. B. Mayor's edition *Thirteen Satires of Juvenal*, Vol. 2, pp. 267-8). Catullus, the mime-writer of Nero's day, wrote a mime called *Phasma* (The Ghost) and the notorious *Laureolus*, in which the actual crucifixion of a bandit was staged. But, nevertheless, the *scurra* seems to have always maintained a certain individuality and the assumption would be that this individuality resided in his special role of *ioculator*. He would indeed be also a *saltator* and skilled in mimetic gesture like the rest of the mime troupe, but his verbal wit would mark him apart from the rest. An inscription of the year A.D. 212 (*CIL* VI.1063), commemorating games put on by an aedile Claudius Gnorimus for some troops, lists among the *acroamata* (entertainments) the names of certain *archimimi* and *stupidi*, together with one Flavius Saturninus as *scurra*. The military connection is interesting, for in Imperial times (see section V) we find the *scurra* more and more in the company of the military. The phenomenon of the amateur *scurra* would surely secure some privileged status for the *scurra* in general. Hence his presence among the military = *Iuventus*. Most significant of all is the fact that in Imperial times the Praetorian Guard bore the nickname *scurrae*, as being employed on Palace duties in Rome itself and so regarded as "Townies".

The mime, established as a literary genre, modelled its characters on those of regular comedy. Ovid writes (*Trist.*2. 497-500):

> *Quid si scripsissem mimos obscena iocantes*
> *qui semper vetiti crimen amoris habent,*
> *in quibus assidue cultus procedit adulter*
> *verbaque dat stulto callida nupta viro?*

> What if I had written mimes with their obscene jests, which always have illicit love as their theme, in which the well-dressed adulterer constantly appears and the clever wife deceives her foolish spouse?

Among the credulous old men, the shrewish matrons, the bold philanderers, the fickle courtesans and the faithless wives, the *scurra*'s role would closely resemble that of the cunning and witty, insolent and abusive *servus callidus* we meet in Plautus.

The marked individuality of the *scurra*'s role as jester would account also for his adoption in an amateur capacity by the Young Men turned *ioculatores*.

It is to be noted however that, before mime at Rome became a play with a plot, we must assume a good measure of individuality for mimetic performers in general. Indeed, even after the literary genre was established, a good deal of the impromptu element remained, as we gather from Cicero's remark in condemning the confusion of evidence in the Caelius trial — *mimi ergo iam exitus, non fabulae; in quo cum clausula non invenitur, fugit aliquis e manibus, dein scabilla concre- pant, aulaeum tollitur* — "And so from then on it's like the end of a mime, not of a regular drama, in which when a proper ending is not to be found, someone escapes arrest, the

castanets rattle, the stage-curtain is raised" (*Cael.*27). The
term *mimus* denotes both performer and performance, which
implies that the genre takes its origin in a one-man entertainment. Before the *mimus* takes to the boards, we shall find him
in the street.

From earliest times Mediterranean cities have known an
animated street life, the favourable climate being conducive
to spending much time out of doors. Business and general
conversation can be conducted in the open. So too can
entertainment. Early Rome knew a variety of street entertainers consisting of acrobats, jugglers, stilt-walkers, imper-
sonators of men and animals, performers with tame bears,
monkeys and dogs. These strolling entertainers were collectively known as *circulatores*, either because they circulated in
the vicinity or because they attracted groups of spectators
(*circuli*). From the references given in *Thes.Ling.Lat.*, s.v. it is
apparent how manifold were the activities of the *circulator*.
The term is used of the public crier (= *praeco*) who read out
magistrates' decrees and also on occasion delivered public
recitals of literary works cf. Plin. *Ep.*4.7.6 *tu hunc luctuosum
Reguli librum ut circulator in foro legeris*, thus augmenting his
salary by the telling of "golden tales" — *assem para et accipe
auream fabulam* (id.2.20.1). In addition to this, he is a conjurer
and illusionist — *circulatorem aspexi equestrem spatham devorasse
ac lanceam in ima viscera condidisse* (Apul. *Metam*.1.4) and the 4th
c. grammarian Victorinus remarks on *circulatores qui animos
hominum sensusque quadam specie veritatis illudunt*, while Ter-
tullian, *Apol.*23 tells us that *magi* (magicians) *multi miracula
circulatoriis praestigiis ludunt*. Habinnas, a guest at Trimalchio's
banquet in Petronius' *Satyricon*, has a clever slave who gives
imitations and recitals. He observes *ego ad circulatores eum
mittendo erudibam. itaque parem non habet, sive muliones volet sive
circulatores imitari; idem sutor est, idem cocus, idem pistor, omnis*

*musae mancipium (Sat.*68.6-7) — "I had him taught by sending him to the *circulatores.* And so he has no equal, whether it be mule-drivers he wants to imitate, or the *circulatores* themselves; he can do a cobbler, a cook, a baker, he is a Jack of All Trades." The boy also recites from Virgil and gives an imitation of trumpeters.

The *circulator* is also a travelling salesman and peddler, going the rounds of markets and fairs, gathering circles of bystanders *(circuli)* and entertaining them with his tricks and anecdotes, in order to sell his goods. What emerges from this is that he is a one-man entertainer and, with his immense repertory of anecdote, sword-swallowing, conjuring, imitation of men and animals, he is a spiritual ancestor of the medieval jongleur. What is more important still for us is that he shares this ancestry with the *mimus* and *scurra,* who also share increasingly in late imperial and medieval times this capacity to stage a one-man performance. It is to be noted that the *scurra* (City wit), the *mimus* as a one-man sketch (as in dramatic *satura?*), the *circulator* and also the *parasitus ridiculus* in Plautus and the cynic beggar philosopher/humorist with whom the *ridiculus* claims affinity in dress at least, are all individuals rather than members of a troupe of players.

We may note also that both Livy and Valerius Maximus imply that Livius Andronicus was a one-man performer — *isque sui operis actor, cum saepius a populo revocatus vocem obtudisset, adhibito pueri ac tibicinis concentu gesticulationem tacitus peregit —* "the performer of his own work, when, because of frequent encores, he had bruised his voice, he made use of the accompaniment of a boy and of a flute-player, and carried through the mimicry in silence". (Val. Max.2.4.4). From this it would appear that even the *fabula* with a plot (Andronicus' innovation) was at first a one-man performance, deriving as it did from the one-man sketch, the *satura (Livius, qui ab saturis*

ausus est primus argumento fabulam serere — Livy 7.2.8). The
dramatic *satura*, as a one-man performance, would be as much
at home on the street pavement as on the boards, and we may
link its *actor* in company with the *circulator* and *scurra* as street
entertainers in origin before the *scurra* mounted the stage in
primitive mime at Rome.

It is certain that the theatrical performances of mime at
Rome contained much knock-about farce and that the
mimetic skill of the players in gesture and facial expression
(they did not wear masks) was enhanced by clownish antics,
such as face-slapping, somersaults, juggling and the like.
This argues for a considerable repertory of skills for each
individual performer. These would be shared by the *scurra*
and indeed there is a fragment of Lucilius the satirist (c. 180-
102 B.C.) which mentions a *scurra* Coelius who was skilled at
quoits, and we are reminded of Plautus' *servi scurrarum in via*
who play ball games to the annoyance of passers-by
(*Curc.*296-7).

Thus it is a fair assumption that the *mimi*, including the
scurrae, of ancient Rome graduated to the stage from the
street. But in what form of primitive dramatic mime did they
make their earliest appearance? One thinks of the early
dramatic sketches called *saturae*, a kind of vaudeville with
burlesqued situations, caricature of persons, singing, music
and mimetic gesture. But we are warned off these, for Livy
tells us that they were performed by *histriones*, professional
Roman players to whom the Etruscan name was given, no
doubt to stress the foreign nature of the importation, still
frowned upon in conservative circles.

An alternative is left to us; we may turn to the *exodia*, comic
sketches which contained the jesting in verse-form practised
by the Young Men in the tradition of the old Fescennine
merrymaking, the verse-form being in all probability the

native Saturnian metre. These *exodia*, Livy tells us, were subsequently embodied into the Atellan farce, which the Young Men adopted as their perquisite, reserving for its players amateur status. It is likely then that the Young Men themselves performed in these *exodia* and that the role they played therein was that of the *ioculator*, in other words the *scurra*. It was thus to my mind that the amateur *scurra* came into being. The Young Men who amused themselves and the public (*deliciae popli*) by playing the *ioculator* in these *exodia* came to be known as *scurrae*.

How is it then that in the pages of Plautus and, as we shall see, in those of Cicero and Horace, the *scurra* is condemned as a social menace, a know-all and a dangerous gossip? It can only be that the *iocularia* overflowed from the stage into real life; that the high-spirited and socially powerful *Iuventus*, who indulged a love of the theatrical in defiance of conservative opinion, began to exercise their satirical spirit at the expense of the community at large. Their temperament was rebellious, at war with convention, and flaunted in public a licence of conduct and of speech.

Now, it is clear from Horace's remarks in *Epistles* 2.1, quoted above, that he accepts what was apparently a traditional view of the "Fescennine licence", namely that it derived from rustic merrymaking which had religious significance and was associated with thanksgiving to personifications of the fertility spirits, such as Mother Earth and Silvanus, supposedly a god of the untilled land, who needs to be propitiated when encroachments are made upon his territory, and who came to be roughly identified with another woodland spirit, Faunus, of prophetic powers, so that he is called *fatuus* — "the speaker". It is likely therefore that the *Iuventus* have this religious significance in mind when indulging their *iocularia*.

Megaronides in Plautus' *Trinummus* (200) refers to the *urbani assidui cives quos scurras vocant* and I suggested that *assiduus* may here = *locuples* or *dives* ("well-to-do"). At any rate, Cicero uses both these latter terms with reference to *scurrae*.

It is not surprising to find that notorious demagogue Publius Clodius, political trouble-maker and rebel against social and religious convention, in the company of the amateur *scurrae*, with whom, following the death of his father, he debauched his youthful years — *qui post patris mortem primam illam aetatulam suam ad scurrarum locupletium libidines detulit* (*de Harus.Resp.*42) — and was in fact their *mignon* — *locupletium scurrarum scortum* (*Sest.*39). Here then Cicero stresses the dissolute aspect of the well-to-do amateur. Clodius was in fact, by his utter disregard for conventional morality, himself a true *scurra*.

The shamelessness here attributed to *scurrae*, worthy of the Cynic ἀναιδής at his worst, is echoed by the unknown author of the *Rhetorica ad Herennium* (c. 85 B.C.) who describes a *scurra* as *exhausto rubore, qui se putaret nihil habere quod de existimatione perderet, ut omnia sine famae detrimento facere posset* — "beyond all capacity for shame, considering that he had nothing to lose in the way of reputation, so that he might do any and everything without further damage to it".

Outrageous conduct has thus become by Cicero's time a marked attribute of the amateur *scurra*. Four specimens are further cited by him — Gnaeus Carbo and his brother — *quid his improbius?* (*ad Fam.*9.21.3), Alba who delights to be considered *scurra improbissimus* (*Verr.*2.3.146) and Quintus Manlius who is *petulans* and *improbus* — "aggressive and shameless" (*Cluent.*39), and who by slander and civil discord had climbed to the tribunate.

Shamelessness alike in domestic and public life is combined with slanderous abuse daily practised in stirring up civil discord and litigation (the *scurrae divitis cottidianum convicium* — *Quinct*.62) in those whom Cicero denounces as amateur *scurrae*. The keynote of their language is *dicacitas*, "sharp-tongued malice", defined by Quintilian as *sermonem cum risu aliquos incessentem* (6.3.21) — "the speech of aggressive mockery". Cicero in his *Orator* points the distinction between *dicax* "abusive" and *facetus* "witty", remarking that Demosthenes is more the latter than the former, the one revealing sharpness of intellect, the other a greater artistry — *Demosthenes non tam dicax fuit quam facetus. Est autem illud acrioris ingenii, hoc maioris artis* (26.90).

A notable example of the amateur *scurra* is Sextus Naevius, a business associate of Caius Quinctius whose brother Publius Cicero defended in a lawsuit (*Pro Quinctio Oratio*). Nature had bestowed upon him a good voice, his father had left him nothing but his free-born status; so he put his voice to work for him and made use of his civil status to be malicious with impunity — *cum ei natura nihil melius quam vocem dedisset, pater nihil praeter libertatem reliquisset, vocem in quaestum contulit, libertate usus est quo impunius dicax esset* (*Quinct*.11). This being his temperament he was irresponsible, both in the sphere of public relations and as regards the duties of family life; he was *non ita institutus ut iura societatis et officia certa patris familiae nosse posset* (ibid.). Such anti-social behaviour proverbially led to riches rather than to family responsibility — *vetus est de scurra multo facilius divitem quam patrem familias fieri posse* (ibid. 55).

Thus, the amateur *scurra* in Cicero is a threat to conventional morality and to political stability, partly because of his restless, demagogic temperament, but mainly on account of his slanderously abusive tongue, so that Cicero firmly rebukes Cato for calling Lucius Murena a vulgar entertainer

— *non debes, M. Cato, adripere maledictum ex trivio aut ex scurrarum aliquo convicio, neque temere consulem populi Romani saltatorem vocare, ... (Mur.*13) — "you ought not, Marcus Cato, to seize upon some insult taken from the gutter or from a *scurra*'s repertory of abuse, nor hastily call a consul of the Roman people a mime performer".

The *scurra* is then for Cicero, as for Plautus, a social menace. We shall now turn to Horace, who mentions both the amateur and the professional *scurra*.

In *Epistles* 1.15 Horace presents us with a sketch of one Maenius who, having exhausted his family inheritance, lives by his malicious wit and has in fact become a parasite, an amateur *scurra* turned semi-professional, the lot of many of his kind throughout the ages:

> *Maenius, ut rebus maternis atque paternis*
> *fortiter absumptis urbanus coepit haberi,*
> *scurra vagus, non qui certum praesepe teneret,*
> *impransus non qui civem dinosceret hoste,*
> *quaelibet in quemvis opprobria fingere saevus,*
> *pernicies et tempestas barathrumque macelli,*
> *quidquid quaesierat ventri donabat avaro.* (26-32)

Maenius, having lost no time in getting through the estate of both father and mother, took on the role of City wit, a vagrant jester with no feeding place to call his own. When short of a meal he made no distinction between friend or foe, savagely prepared to invent any kind of abuse against anyone. A veritable storm and tempest, a yawning gulf in the provision market, whatever came his way he would bestow upon his hungry belly.

A similar sketch of a *scurra dicax* is presented in *Sermones* 1.4.81-5:

> *absentem qui rodit amicum*
> *qui non defendit alio culpante, solutos*
> *qui captat risus hominum famamque dicacis,*
> *fingere qui non visa potest, commissa tacere*
> *qui nequit; hic niger est, hunc tu, Romane, caveto.*

He who backbites an absent friend, omitting to defend him when another attacks him, seeking only the applause of laughter and a reputation for mordant wit. He invents things he has not seen for himself and cannot keep secrets entrusted to him. Beware, O Roman, of this man, for he is a poisonous fellow.

The implication is that no one at Rome, even the free-born citizen, is safe from the *scurra*'s malice, for the amateur has become a semi-professional and earns his bread at the patron's table with his wicked tongue. In him we see the makings of the *delator*, the informer, the scourge of Imperial times often found in the ranks of Court favourites. Horace's "Beware of this man, O Roman" has a prophetic significance. The phrase *fingere qui non visa potest* reminds us of Megaronides' *quae neque futura neque sunt, tamen illi sciunt* (*Trin.*209). The type has not changed since Plautus' day, except perhaps that he is descending in the social scale — the *urbanus assiduus civis* has degenerated from the amateur ne'er-do-well to the impoverished hanger-on, the *scurra vagus* whom we shall increasingly encounter.

Scurrilia are in fact falling more and more into disrepute and Horace warns his friend Scaeva, who is anxious to cultivate the powerful, not to sink to the parasite's level, but to temper flattering jests with independence. He cites

(*Ep*.1.17) the example of Aristippus, friend of Socrates and at the same time an advocate of pleasurable living who did not scorn to cultivate the rich. When taunted by Diogenes the Cynic that the true way to satisfy one's natural needs was to practise frugality, Aristippus retorted that to gain a comfortable living by pleasing rich patrons was a means of achieving independence for one's jesting. Horace makes him say (*Ep*.1.17.19) *scurror ipse mihi, populo tu* — "I do my jesting for myself alone, you have to please an audience".

Similarly, in his next Epistle, Horace warns his outspoken friend Lollius not to degenerate into a parasitic *scurra* by abject flattery of patrons, nor yet to become offensively rude in a show of independence —

> *Si bene te novi, metues, liberrime Lolli,*
> *scurrantis speciem praebere, professus amicum.*
> *ut matrona meretrici dispar erit atque*
> *discolor, infido scurrae distabit amicus.*

> (*Ep*.1.18.1-4)

> If I know you well, my outspoken Lollius, you will
> guard against appearing to be a mere *scurra*, while
> professing to be a friend. Just as a respectable matron
> will look different and indeed wear a different coloured
> dress from the courtesan, so will a friend be
> distinguishable from the teacherous *scurra*.

From the examples quoted above, it would hardly seem that the Young Men About Town, Livy's *Iuventus*, the *urbani cives* of Plautus, the socially well-born like Publius Clodius, in spite of his left-wing proclivities, or the politically ambitious Sextus Naevius and Quintus Manlius, the *scurrae locupletes*, would care to be numbered with mere wastrels like Maenius or the types against whom Horace warns his friends. The latter have sunk to a level which puts them on a par with the professional parasite jesters like Peniculus, Ergasilus and Gelasimus whom we met in Plautus, the *imi subselli viri* of Cynic beggar-philosopher tradition. The *scurra locuples* prefers Aristippus' way to that of Diogenes, to achieve a comfortable, indeed luxurious existence rather than a frugal competence by choosing his rich patrons wisely and keeping a measure of independence (*scurror ipse mihi*). It would seem that by Horace's time this was becoming increasingly difficult for the by now thoroughly discredited *scurra* to do.

Horace's reference in *Epistles* 1.17 to the exchange between Aristippus and Diogenes — *si pranderet holus patienter, regibus uti nollet Aristippus: si sciret regibus uti, fastidiret holus qui me notat* (13-15) — "if he could bear to dine on plain vegetables, Aristippus would not wish to cultivate patrons: if he who thus criticizes me knew how to make use of patrons, he would despise a vegetable diet", — pinpoints the distinction between the amateur *scurra*, whom we have met in the pages of Plautus and Cicero and who, like Aristippus, indulges in *scurrilia* largely for his own amusement, in response to his own fractious temperament, and the professional *scurra*, the needy, vagrant parasite whose jests earn him a precarious livelihood in the humblest place at a patron's dinner-table.

Moreover, it would seem that, by Horace's time, the professional *scurra* is to be linked with the Cynic beggar philosopher, who is also an *imi subselli vir*. He has then, by this time, been relegated to the position of the *parasiti ridiculi* of Plautus, who were also, by their dress and language, to be associated with the Cynic tradition of humour. But Plautus does not refer to Gelasimus and company as *scurrae*; the latter are all well-to-do Young Men About Town, ex-patrons of the *ridiculi*, and their own cult of *iocularia* has led them to dispense with the services of professional jesters.

The process we see as having taken place between Plautus' time and Horace's is a natural and inevitable one. The vogue for *iocularia* as a social accomplishment, initiated by the *Iuventus* mentioned by Livy and glimpsed in Plautus, has grown to the extent that the parasitic stratum of Roman society is largely composed of would-be *scurrae urbani*. At the same time, the odium resulting from the harmful effects upon society of the malicious scandal-mongering which is the hallmark of *scurrilia*, an odium of which Cicero makes us fully aware and for which Megaronides' remarks in Plautus had prepared us, must have a discouraging effect upon the amateur *ioculator*, so that he no longer wishes to be associated with the *scurra vagus* whom we meet in Horace and whom I have called professional. Indeed I think it can safely be said that we do not meet with the truly amateur *scurra* other than in Plautus and Cicero. Catullus' Suffenus, the witty companion but indifferent poet, may seem like a *scurra* (22.12) but surely aspires to higher social esteem.

This much said, one must not lose sight of the fact that the term *scurra* is theatrical, that the *scurra* is in origin a mime performer, a *saltator/ioculator*. This then is his true professional capacity and we cannot identify the mime actor with the *scurra vagus*, the individual jester at the rich man's table. We must rather suppose that the degenerate *scurra* derives from the well-to-do amateur, in other words that the hiving-off of *scurrilia* from the professional theatre is due entirely to the initiative of the Roman *Iuventus* whose interest in the early Theatre at Rome led them to adopt *iocularia* for their own purposes.

It would be better then to call the hanger-on at the rich

man's table, who has fallen in with the beggar Cynic and with Plautus' *ridiculi*, a *semi-professional scurra* when he exercises his jests for the entertainment of the guests.

I now turn to an important passage in Horace. *Sermones* 1.5 is an account of a journey from Rome to Brundisium and is modelled upon a similar account written by the satirist Lucilius. Horace is travelling in the company of his patron Maecenas and other notables, including Maecenas' brother-in-law, Lucius Fonteius Capito and Marcus Cocceius Nerva, both ex-consuls. The seventh night of their journey is spent at Cocceius' villa, beyond Caudium in Samnium. An entertainment for the guests is provided by a contest of wit between a *scurra* named Sarmentus and one Messius who is called a *cicirrus*, a word meaning "cock" according to Hesychius (*Lexic.* ed. Latte, κ 2647) and cf. *Auct. Carm. Philom.* 25 *cucurrire solet gallus, gallina gracillat*. Sarmentus is an ex-slave, whose former mistress, Horace tells us, is still alive, but he has been freed by Maecenas, into whose possession he had passed, and is now employed in his suite as a secretary. But for the present occasion he is acting as a *scurra*, so that clearly we may regard him as a semi-professional, no doubt rewarded with a gratuity for his evening's work. Here then we have an interesting example of a non-theatrical *scurra*, a man whose natural talent for witty repartee enables him to assume the jester's role.

Messius the *cicirrus* is described as an Oscan and presumably he belongs to Cocceius' household at Caudium, for Samnium was in Oscan territory. But it is not impossible that it is also implied that he was a (semi-professional?) Atellan player, for the Atellan farce was a product of Oscan civilisation.

Horace gives us a sample of the exchange between these two (56-69): Sarmentus begins "I declare that you look like a wild horse" (*equi te esse feri similem dico*). The audience laughs and Messius accepts the role and tosses his head. "If you hadn't had the horn cut off from your forehead," continues Sarmentus, "what would you be doing, since, although mutilated, you still make threatening gestures?" (*O, tua cornu ni foret exsecto frons, quid faceres, cum sic mutilus minitaris?*) In fact Messius bore an ugly scar on the left side of his head, the relic of a growth known as the Campanian (Oscan) disease, probably consisting of horn-like excrescences, which prompts Sarmentus now to invite Messius to do a Cyclops dance in the manner of a horned satyr goat-herd; he could do without the comic mask and tragic buskins. The reference here is to the parodic dance of the satyr-play which burlesqued the situations of tragedy.

It is now Messius' turn; he taunts Sarmentus with his past as a slave. Apparently he had run away from his mistress and been put in chains for it. But why ever had he run away — his smallness and his thinness show that he had been content with meagre fare?

This brief encounter suggests that such impromptu entertainments were common at Roman social gatherings in Horace's day and that the scurrile tradition of humour could meet on common ground with the Atellan and satyric traditions (the two latter are linked by later grammarians who equate the *fabula Atellana* of Italy with the Greek *fabula satyrica*; cf. Diomedes, *Ars Gram*.III (= Keil, *Gramm.Lat*.I p. 490) — *Atellanae, argumentis dictisque iocularibus similes satyricis fabulis Graecis*).

Had Horace favoured us with more details of the encounter we might have gathered valuable information about the nature of such entertainments. As it is we note that animal impersonation is a feature of them, recalling both the stage mime and the street entertainer; for the *scurra* as animal imitator and ventriloquist cf. Phaedrus, *Fab*.5.5 (*Scurra et Rusticus*), 7-19.

> *venere artifices laudis ad certamina,*
> *quos inter scurra, notus urbano sale.*
> . . .
> *ille in sinum repente demisit caput,*
> *et sic porcelli vocem imitatus sua,*
> *verum ut subesse pallio contenderent*
> *et excuti iuberent* [sc. *spectatores*].

> Players came along to the contest, among them a *scurra*, noted for his urbane wit . . . who, suddenly putting his head beneath his cloak, so imitated a pig with his voice that the onlookers claimed that he had a real pig under his garment and demanded that he shake it out.

The Cyclops dance invokes the satyr-plays, in particular the *Cyclops* of Euripides, in which the chorus mimics the antics of the one-eyed giants worsted by Odysseus. These things are performed by Messius. Is he in the Atellan tradition and does his nickname of "cock" indicate an animal portrayal associated with that tradition?

It is disappointing that more is not made of Sarmentus as a *scurra*. He has been a runaway slave and one recalls that Juvenal (13.111) mentions a mime by Catullus (of Nero's reign) in which a *scurra* plays the part of a *servus fugitivus*. Perhaps already before Catullus wrote, this was a stock part for mime, in which case Plautus' *servi callidi* may owe something to this type of role, for their abusive wit and ready repartee has much of the scurrile spirit.

Horace refers twice to a *scurra* Pantolabus (Take-all) in *Sermones* 1.8.11 and 2.1.22. The name suggests an entertainer, but he is put in the company on both occasions with one Nomentanus who is described as *nepos*, a "spendthrift", and who is presumably another Maenius. Both characters may come from Lucilius. Both, says Horace, are likely to end up in the common burial ground for paupers on the Campus Esquilinus, the subject of 1.8. Nomentanus is also mentioned in 1.1.102, 2.3.175 and 224, and is evidently proverbial as a waster of his inheritance — an amateur *scurra* turned semi-professional.

V

The Scurra *in the* Historia Augusta *and in the Church Councils*

The most striking fact about the *scurra* is his longevity — the persistent recurrence of a name of which the derivation is unknown and the precise meaning obscure. It would seem that as long as Latin continued to be the normal medium of official communication the word *scurra* continued to appear. This can only mean that the personage represented by the word continued to exist in the society in whose documents he was mentioned, so that although the name was obscure the personage was real. When Richard Croke, tutor to Henry VIII's natural son the Duke of Richmond, complained to Wolsey that too much encouragement was given in the boy's entourage to *scurrae et mimi* (see E. K. Chambers, *The Medieval Stage*, Oxford 1903, Vol. I, p. 68, note 2), it is clear that they constituted the same kind of moral and social threat as in the time of Plautus, Cicero and Horace.

We saw that Maecenas and his friends watched the contest between the *scurra* Sarmentus and the *cicirrus* Messius, and that the *scurra* in Phaedrus' fable was a ventriloquist and animal impersonator. It was then the fashion in Augustus' and Tiberius' reigns to be so entertained. Almost certainly Caligula would have watched them, since he eagerly affected the *scaenicas saltandi canendique artes* (Suet. *Calig.*26), and Tacitus tells us that Uncle Claudius meanwhile sought their company (*cum privatus olim conversatione scurrarum iners otium* *oblectaret — Ann.*12.49.1). The mime writer Catullus who flourished under Caligula made his *scurra* play the part of a runaway slave, as we learn from Juvenal 13.110 *mimum agit ille,/urbani qualem fugitivus scurra Catulli.* Presumably, this *scurra* played the part of a *servus callidus*, insolent and witty in the Plautine manner, as well as being on the run for his misdemeanours. For the *scurra* is always to be distinguished from the other *mimi* by his *iocularia.* The younger Pliny employed entertainers to amuse his guests and more than once refers to *lectores, lyristae* and *comoedi.* But he has no liking *si quid molle a cinaedo, petulans a scurra, stultum a morione profertur* (*Ep.*9.17.2) — "the effeminacies of the pervert, the peevishness of the *scurra*, the stupidities of the fool". Quintilian, writing in Domitian's reign, remarks on the subject of laughter — *cum videatur autem res levis et quae ab scurris, mimis, insipientibus denique saepe moveatur, tamen habet vim nescio an imperiosissimam et cui repugnari minime potest* (*Inst.Orat.*6.3.8) from which we see that the *scurrae* and *mimi* are separate categories of personage. The distinction is maintained throughout imperial and medieval Latin literature. At the same time the frequent use of the term *scurra mimicus* implies that the individual, amateur City wit is still to be found in these later times and not to be confused and identified with his theatrical opposite number.

Passing from Quintilian and the first century, we can discover a number of interesting references to the *scurra* of the second and third centuries, to be found in the *Historia Augusta.*

The account of the life of Lucius Verus, co-Emperor with Marcus Aurelius from 161 until his death in 169, tells us that he brought back from Syria and the Parthian War *fidicinas et tibicines et histriones scurrasque mimarios et praestigiatores . . . prorsus ut videretur bellum non Parthicum sed histrionicum confecisse*

— "harpists, flute-players, actors, mime-jesters and jugglers
... so that altogether it seemed that he had concluded a war,
not against Parthians but against players" (*Hist.Aug.Verus*
8.11 — all references to the *Scriptores Historiae Augustae* are
taken from the Loeb edition by David Magie). Here then,
actors and mime-jesters are linked together (*histriones scurrasque* ...), but identified as separate kinds of entertainer,
while the epithet *mimarius* shows that *scurrae* belong to mime
but are not simply *mimi*. Incidentally, the passage reminds us
of Plautus' *Stichus* where Gelasimus the *parasitus ridiculus* is
delighted to learn that his patron Epignomus has returned
from his Asian war laden with treasure and *fidicinas, tibicinas,
sambucas ... forma eximia*, only to be dismayed a moment later
by the news that the master has also brought along *parasitos
... ridiculissimos* (*Stich.*380-9).

Marcus Aurelius was succeeded by his son Commodus
(180-192) who, from his earliest years, resembled Nero in his
corrupt tastes and indulgence of theatrical hangers-on — *nam
a prima statim pueritia turpis, improbus, crudelis, libidinosus, ore
quoque pollutus et constupratus fuit. iam in his artifex, quae stationis
imperatoriae non erant, ut calices fingeret, saltaret, cantaret,
sibilaret, scurram denique et gladiatorem perfectum ostenderet*
(*Comm.*1.7-8) — "from childhood he was depraved, cruel,
lustful and foul-mouthed. Then too he was a skilled performer in things unbecoming his imperial status, pot-making[?],
dancing, singing, whistling, clowning and playing at
gladiators[?]" — *scurram denique* resumes the accomplishments listed and suggests a varied repertoire. *Gladiatorem* is
here a derogatory term, (cf. Cic. *Cat.*2.4.7: *quis veneficus, quis
gladiator, quis latro, quis sicarius* etc. applied to associates of
Catiline) and means something like "desperado", but in
Commodus' case there is probably an allusion to his convic-
tion that he was an incarnation of Hercules and to his

decision to appear in public in gladiatorial costume on the first of January 193, an event forestalled by his murder the day before.

Following the brief reigns and assassinations of Pertinax and Didius Iulianus (Jan.-June 193), Septimius Severus gained the throne. Shortly before his death at York (4 Feb. 211) following unsuccessful raids into Scotland, an event occurred near Carlisle which was taken to be an omen of his imminent demise. During an inspection of fortifications he was met by an Aethiopian soldier, well known as a jester, who presented him with a cypress garland (a token of mourning) and addressed him. The Latin runs (*Sev.*22.4-5) *Aethiops quidam e numero militari clarae inter scurras famae et celebratorum semper iocorum cum corona e cupressu facta eidem occurrit: "Totum fuisti, totum vicisti, iam deus esto victor"* — "You have lived completely, you have conquered completely, from now, O Victor, be a god", signifying no doubt that it was time for Severus to become a deified (i.e. dead) Emperor.

Here then is an example of the witty, pointed and malicious jesting typical of the *scurra* of tradition. It is interesting to note also that the *scurra* of this context is to be found among the military (*e numero militari*). The Praetorian Guard, since they were stationed close to Rome itself and were employed largely as bodyguards to the Imperial family, were nicknamed *scurrae*, the implication being that they were "Townies", *urbani* and might be supposed to have acquired something of the wit and polish of the *scurra urbanus*. The Emperor Elagabalus (218-222) was murdered by the Guard — *occisus est per scurras* is the phrase (*Elag.*33.7). His successor, the well-meaning Severus Alexander (222-235), was equally their victim, as we read (*unus ex Germanis qui scurrarum officium sustinebat* (i.e. as bodyguard) *ad contubernales suos venit* *eosque ad durum principem interimendum cohortatus est* (*Sev.Alex.*61.3-5). Presumably also there is the implication in the nickname that the City garrison are softened by easy living. The same reproach is made by Thesprio, the servant of the soldier Stratippocles, to Plautus' Epidicus, the Town House slave — *scurra es*, to which Epidicus retorts — *scio te esse equidem hominem militarem* — "a military man, fit from recent active service" (*Epid.*15-16).

Severus Alexander's successor was the giant centurion Maximinus (235-238). His death, like that of Septimius Severus, was foretold by a *scurra*, this time in the theatre. He spoke in Greek verse of which, says the chronicler, the Latin sense was (*Maxim. Duo* 9.4):

> *et qui ab uno non potest occidi, a multis occiditur.*
> *elephans grandis est et occiditur;*
> *leo fortis est et occiditur;*
> *tigris fortis est et occiditur.*
> *cave multos, si singulos non times.*

> He who cannot be killed by one, is killed by many. The elephant is big and he is killed; the lion and the tiger are brave and they are killed. Beware of the many, if you do not fear individuals.

Maximinus was a man of great size and strength who behaved with much brutality, apparently believing himself invincible and immortal like his predecessor Commodus, the incarnation of Hercules. Apparently he did not understand the *scurra*'s remarks which in any case, he was told, were not meant personally. For us they serve as an example of the innuendo we associate with the *scurra mimicus* but of which we have all too few examples.

The Emperor Gallienus (253-268), unjustly maligned by his biographer "Trebellius Pollio" who claimed that he cared for little except feasting and entertainment, was also murdered by his bodyguard. Among other more pertinent reasons for his assassination, he appears to have enraged his soldiery by his atrocious treatment of certain *scurrae* whom he burnt alive for their indiscreet wit. On one triumphant occasion a band of Persian captives were being led along when they were accosted by the *scurrae* (normally a part of triumphal processions), who pretended to scan the faces of the prisoners with intense curiosity. When asked why, they replied "We are searching for the Emperor's father" (*Gall*.9.5). The exact point of the jest, if such it be, is lost to us, but it is a fact that Gallienus' father Valerian had been betrayed to the Persians and had died in captivity.

Gallienus, like his predecessor Claudius, appears to have had a constant need for the company of *scurrae* along with his concubines — *mensam secundam scurrarum et mimorum semper prope habuit* (*Gall*.17.7). Again we see the two categories of entertainer linked but distinct in identity. Their presence denotes low-living and debauchery, the atmosphere of the mime itself at Rome. Gallienus' son Salonius who met his death in 259 spent his nights in taverns with low company — *semper noctibus popinas dicitur frequentasse et cum lenonibus, mimis scurrisque vixisse* (*Gall*.21.6).

Gallienus' successor Claudius II (268-270) had trouble with a pretender Censorinus whom some supported and declared Emperor. He was lame and jestingly called Claudius — *scurrarum ioco Claudius appellatus est* (*Tyr.XXX*.33) with a play on the word *claudus* and with a hint at the first Claudius who also was lame. Indeed, the *scurrae* here mentioned may be guardsmen rather than jesters, for the first Claudius had been hailed as Emperor by the Praetorians, more in jest than in earnest, until the idea took on.

The next Emperor, Aurelian (270-275), was described by

"Vopiscus" as one of the very few good Emperors — *vide,
quaeso, quam pauci sint principes boni, ut bene dictum sit a quodam
mimico scurra Claudii huius temporibus in uno anulo bonos principes
posse perscribi atque depingi (Aurel.42.5)* — "see, I beg you,
how few are the good Emperors, so that it was well said by a
certain jester of the time of this Claudius [i.e. the second] that
the good Emperors could be written down and even
portrayed upon a single ring".

Aurelian defeated and captured Queen Zenobia of Pal-
myra whose conquests had threatened the West. She was led
in his triumph, magnificently dressed and weighed down
with jewels and with a chain of gold about her neck so heavy
that it was partly supported by a Persian *scurra (Tyr.XXX.
33.26)*. Was he a soldier or an entertainer or both?

Not the least interesting characteristic of the *scurra* is his
individuality. We have seen how he is given a distinct
identity in the collocation *mimi scurraeque*; in the professional
mime troupe he has a strongly individual role; he is not just a
saltator in dumb-show with skilled technique in *gestus vul-
tusque* but he is also vocal as a *ioculator*. It is this vocal role
which enables him to be an individual. For it gives him the
opportunity to improvise, to seize upon the unexpected
incident or encounter and to invent a witty response. It is this
individuality, this spontaneity which begets the amateur,
the malicious gossip, the witty young man about Town,
the ruined profligate or the talented slave turned semi-
professional, the *parasitus ridiculus* both hereditary and newly
trained. Maecenas' ex-slave Sarmentus is a clerk in his service
but when occasion demands he is a *scurra*, able to compete
with the presumably Atellan *cicirrus* to entertain guests.
Already then, at the beginning of the imperial age, we have
the entertainer established as an essential component of
wealthy households. We remember half a century later Pliny

the Younger's *histrio* Zosimus of great virtuosity and Ummidia's personal team of *pantomimi* (*Ep.*5.19 and 7.24), and the *Historia Augusta* has shown us the beginnings of that royal patronage which will culminate in the establishment of the medieval Court Jester.

The individuality, the capacity to improvise can make a *scurra* of any discontented, dispossessed, restless temperament endowed with a quick wit and the desire to express grievance and a sense of injustice with carping criticism and malicious innuendo. And so, by the end of the imperial age and moving from the pagan to the Christian scene, we find frequent references to *scurrae* and *scurrilia* in the pronouncements of the Church Councils. Already at the Council of Carthage in 436 we find the directive that the *clericum scurrilem et verbis turpibus iocularem ab officio retrahendum* (Mansi, *Concilia* 3.956), an injunction frequently repeated in succeeding centuries (e.g. Narbonne in 506, Toledo in 694). The early monastic rules and the writings of the Church Fathers condemn *scurrilia* and *risus multus vel excussus* (see P. B. Corbett, "Unidentified Source Material common to *Regula Magistri, Regula Benedicti* and *Regula IV Patrum?*", in *Regula Benedicti Studia*, Vol. V (1976) pp. 27-31) but there is more to it than misbehaviour in church or cloister. The church and the cloister confer many privileges and exemptions and attract many recruits. Inevitably many of these find that they are temperamentally unsuited to the discipline and austerity required of the religious life. They break the monotony by idle conversation, give voice to complaints and bitter remarks of disillusionment. They are denounced by authority as *scurrae* and are banished, becoming not only *scurrae* but *vagi* as well — a tribe which will increase alarmingly through the centuries.

I began this section by remarking on the longevity of the

name *scurra*, the more striking in view of the obscurity of the derivation. Certainly its use in medieval Latin documents is a left-over from classical times. However, the *scurra* is essentially and predominantly a *ioculator*, so that inevitably we find in medieval phraseology the collocation *mimi scurraeque* replaced on occasion by *mimi ioculatoresque*. Thus, while Theganus, in his Life of Louis the Pious (814-840) (= *MGH, SS* 2.594), tells us that the Emperor refused to display his white teeth in a smile when *in summis festivitatibus ad laetitiam populi procedebant thymelici* ["musicians"], *scurrae et mimi*, Agobert, writing in 836 in his *Liber de dispensatione rerum ecclesiasticarum*, speaks of *mimos turpissimosque et vanissimos ioculatores* (= *MGH, Ep. V.S*.178). Gradually *ioculator* will gain in frequency as it is immediately intelligible whereas *scurra* is not, and so *ioculator* via its derivative *iocular(em)* has given us ioglar, ioglier, jougleor, juggler and many variants, notably the French jongleur, whereas *scurra* has not survived into the vernacular tongues.

The medieval term jongleur of course embraces a much greater range of achievement than that of the *scurra/ioculator* — it covers the recital of epic verse and narrative tale, of lives of saints, bawdy songs, witty satire and amorous anecdote, song, dance, acrobatics, animal impersonation, entertainment at every intellectual level for all levels of society, as the many variants imply — *mimi, histriones, salii, balatrones, aemiliani, gladiatores, palaestritae, gignardii, praestigiatores, bufones, eberhardini, trutanni, leccatores, ribaldi, goliardi*, etc., the precise meanings of which are obscure, so that their distinctive functions can only be conjectured. The lower ranks of these entertainers would be street and fairground performers, only occasionally summoned to the houses of the great, but the talented and cultivated artists often became permanently attached to the Court of prince or bishop and were distinguished by the more prestigious title of *menestral* and other derivatives of the Latin *ministralis* — civil servant or court official. (See on the medieval jongleur E. Faral, *Les Jongleurs en France au Moyen-Age*, Paris 1964, and Enid Welsford, *The Fool*, London 1968.)

To confine ourselves to the *scurra*, since the jongleur has been fully treated many times, we note that Duke Robert of Normandy, son of William the Conqueror, like the Emperor Gallienus and his son, sought the company of mistresses and mimes and, like many before him, demolished his inheritance in such living — *meretricum atque scurrarum consortia non refutavit sed eis impudenter applaudens sua dilapidavit* (Orderic Vitalis, *Hist.Eccl.*X.iv.105 = M. Chibnall, ed., *Oxford Med. Texts*, Vol. V, 1975, p. 308) and we are reminded of Publius Clodius who *primam illam aetatulam suam ad scurrarum locupletium libidines detulit* (Cic. *Harusp.Resp.*42). Serlo of Bayeux, Bishop of Séez in Normany ca. 1100, indignantly relates how these creatures rob Robert of his very clothing — *scurrae nimirum et meretrices quae illum frequenter comitantur, vestes eius, dum ebrietate madens stertit, noctu furantur, et cum cachinnis sese ducem spoliasse gloriantur* (Vitalis, XI.iv.206 = Chibnall Vol. VI p. 62). Salonius found his pimps and players in the taverns (*Gall.*21.6) and so did the misguided *clerici* of the 13th century — the Lateran Council of 1215 warns them away from the pubs: *mimis ioculatoribus* [i.e. *scurris*] *et histrionibus non intendant et tabernas prorsus evitent, nisi in itinere, . . . ad aleas vel taxillos non ludant* — "let them not give heed to mimes, jesters and players and avoid taverns altogether, except when travelling[!], . . . let them not play at dice or knucklebones" (Mansi, *Concilia* 22.1003). Some *scurrae* are famous as drinkers, like the tap-room champion in Lambert of Ardre's *Chronicon*, who could drink off a whole cask (*Hist. Comit. Ghisnensium* 124 = *MGH, SS.* 24.622). Three hundred years before an ecclesiastical canon runs — *docemus ut nullus sacerdos fiat cerevisiarius nec aliquo modo scurram agat secum ipso vel aliis* — "we instruct that no priest is to be a beer-fancier [publican?] or to play the clown, either by himself or with others" (Mansi, 18A, 517).

It was all too easy for the disgraced or dispossessed medieval cleric to become a *scurra*. He was not permitted by virtue of his sacred calling to engage in trade. The Lateran Council in the 13th century said *clerici officia vel commercia saecularia non exerceant* (Mansi, 22.1003) and was simply repeating Carthage in the 4th which said *clerici ... neque ullo turpi vel inhonesto negotio victum quaerant* — "the clergy must not seek a livelihood in any base or dishonest business" (Mansi, 3.883). But he had to live somehow. What more natural and obvious than to use and adapt those skills his vocation had taught him? He had learnt to read and write in the monastery scriptorium, to sing and perhaps play a musical instrument as part of the liturgy. So now, in order to eat, he would learn to dance and gesticulate, to compose and sing humorous speech and verse — in a word *scurram agere*.

Horace refers to the *scurra* as *vagus* (*Ep.*1.15), the epithet most commonly applied to the disaffected cleric of the middle ages, as also to his secular brother, the *vagus scholaris*. The three as a temperament are one and their names and attributes indistinguishable, as we read in the injunctions of the Council of Salzburg (1291) — *praecipimus quod clerici non sint ioculatores, goliardi seu bufones, declarantes quod, si per annum illam artem diffamatoriam* [= *scurrilem*] *exercuerint, omni privilegio ecclesiastico sint nudati* — "We order that the clergy must not be jesters, goliards or buffoons; if they pursue such disgraceful accomplishments for a whole year, they are to be stripped of all ecclesiastical privileges." Sorrowfully the Council admits that although *contra quosdam sub vagorum scholarium nomine discurrentes, scurriles, maledicos, blasphemos, adulationibus* *importune vacantes, qui se clericos in vituperium clericalis ordinis profitentur, nonnulla pio zelo pro salubri eorum correctione emana- verint instituta* — "against individuals disporting themselves as wandering scholars, who are really gossips, slanderers, blasphemers and flatterers, and who call themselves clerics to the disgrace of the calling, certain measures have been forthcoming as salutary correction" — yet they do not mend their ways! (Mansi, 24.1017-77). Not only are they clowns, parasites and scandal-mongers, but they *publice nudi incedunt, in furnis* [brothels] *iacent, tabernas, ludos et meretrices frequentant, peccatis suis victum sibi emunt.*

We will leave the *scurra* with the early 14th century account by Thomas Cobham, Bishop of Worcester, in which he says — *sunt etiam alii* [sc. *histriones*] *qui nihil operantur sed criminose agunt, non habentes certum domicilium* — "there are other players who do no work and behave culpably, having no fixed abode" (cf. Hor. *Ep.*1.15.28 *scurra vagus, non qui certum praesepe teneret*) — *sed sequuntur curias magnatum et dicunt opprobria* [cf. ibid. 30 *opprobria fingere saevus*] *et ignominias de absentibus* [cf. *Serm.*1.4.81 *absentem qui rodit amicum*] *ut placeant aliis* — "they frequent the courts of the powerful and utter abuse and slander about absent people to amuse those present"; *dicuntur tales scurrae vagi, quia ad nihil utiles sunt, nisi ad devorandum et maledicendum.* (See E. K. Chambers, *The Medieval Stage*, Vol. II, p. 262.)

So Thomas' *scurrae* are really simply greedy parasites and scandal-mongers and do not deserve to be called *histriones* for they do not do their job. It would seem that the amateur or semi-professional was always to be found, for Thomas' denunciation can hardly have been a mere reminiscence of Plautus and Horace. The *scurra* was as much a temperament as a character of drama, *vagus* as much as *mimicus*, but *urbanus* in both capacities.

In late imperial times and into the middle ages and beyond the word *scurra* signifies an entertainer, not clearly distinguishable from the *mimus, histrio, ludio* and the many other terms employed by the chroniclers and the legislators of church and monastery. Certainly he is a mime performer (*scurra mimicus*) and therefore sometimes described as a *saltator* (*scurra saltas fabulam*). But when we consider the witticisms attributed to him, we see that the *scurra* is really a *ioculator*, that he is essentially vocal, in fact he is probably the protagonist of mime. The confusion of these two constituents of mime, *ioculatio* and *saltatio*, is amusingly illustrated by the fact that Jerome in his Latin version of II Kings 6.20 (Michal's indignant outburst at David's unbecoming behaviour when the Ark was brought into the City) renders the Greek καθὼς ἀποκαλύπτεται ἀποκαλυφθεὶς εἷς τῶν ὀρχουμένων — "he uncovers himself like one of the naked dance performers", by *nudatus est quasi si nudetur unus de scurris*, while the compiler of the 8th century Reichenau Glossary elucidating the same text notes *scurris* (sic) = *ioculator* (*Die Reichenauer Glossen*, ed. H. W. Klein, Munich 1968, Teil I, p. 97).

In Plautus and Cicero, however, we get a different picture. Here the *scurra* is not a mime performer but an *urbanus assiduus civis*, City-wit, busybody and malicious gossip (Plautus) or a ne'er-do-well, spendthrift and troublemaker, the *scurra locuples* or *dives* (Cicero). The theatrical *scurra* of course already exists in the second and first centuries B.C. and is glimpsed in Grumio the country slave's retort to the Townie Tranio — *tu urbanus scurra, deliciae popli* (*Most.*15). (Some four centuries later, in the time of Diocletian, the people of Antinous in Egypt protested to the Prefect Arianus against the condemnation to death of the Christian mime player Philemon with the words: *ne perdas civitatis nostrae delicias*! — see H. Reich,

Der Mimus, p. 180, quoting from *Acta Sanct.* ed. Bollandus, Brussels 1853, Vol. VII, 752 B.)

The *urbani cives* are called *scurrae*, as Megaronides tells us (*Trin.*202). They are then amateur *scurrae*. So which comes first — the theatrical performer or the City-wit, the Man about Town? Being an amateur suggests that there is a previously existing professional; the City-wit is then aping the theatrical *scurra* and his laughter-raising gossip. But the aim of mime is to imitate real life and so the *scurra mimicus* must be imitating the real thing! Obviously, the two exist side by side; the carping temperament is to be found in society at large and also upon the boards, the one causes domestic strife, public scandal and is a dangerous enemy, as Horace warns, the other raises more or less harmless laughter, perhaps an unfortunate stimulus to emulation among those in the audience of similar mischievous inclination.

Thus we find recorded in Latin literature the *scurra urbanus*, the *scurra mimicus* and also the *scurra vagus*, the semi-professional whose natural gift for malice earns him a place at the rich man's table to amuse the guests with current scandal and innuendo at the expense of those absent — Horace's *absentem qui rodit amicum*.

For contexts and definitions of *scurra* consult, in addition to the Oxford Latin Dictionary, Forcellini-De Vit: *Totius Latinitatis Lexicon* and Pauly-Wissowa: *Real-Encyclopädie*, s.v.

The best account of the *scurra* is that of Otto Ribbeck in his "Agroikos" (*Abhandlungen d. königl. sächs. Gesellschaft der Wissenschaften*, philol. hist. Classe, Bd. 10, Leipzig, Hirzel 1888) pp. 55-66, but see also Paul Lejay: *Oeuvres d'Horace*, Paris, Hachette 1911, pp. 551-553 for a lively discussion and some criticism of Ribbeck.

A major work on mime and mime-players, with copious footnotes of source material, is Reich, Hermann: *Der Mimus*, Berlin, Weidmann 1903, especially chapter 2, "Mime in the classical period" and chapter 9, "Mime in the middle ages". Reich, however, does not attempt to define the *scurra*'s distinctive role.

The parasite in ancient comedy is discussed in Fraenkel, Eduard: *Elementi Plautini in Plauto*, Firenze, "La Nuova Italia", 1972, especially p. 182f. and 236f., and by Handley, E. W. ed.: *The Dyskolos of Menander*, London, Methuen, 1965, p. 140f. and by Gomme, A. W. and Sandbach, F. H.: *Menander, a commentary*, Oxford 1973, p. 131f. and 420f.

On the medieval jester, useful accounts are given by: Chambers, E. K.: *The Medieval Stage*, 2 vols. Oxford 1903; Faral, Edmond: *Les Jongleurs en France au Moyen-Age*, Paris, Champion 1964; Nykrog, Per: *Les Fabliaux*, Genève, Droz 1973; Schreier-Hornung, Antonie: *Spielleute, Fahrende, Aussenseiter,* Göppingen, Kümmerle Verlag 1981; Welsford,

Enid: *The Fool*, London, Faber, 1968, to which we may add the detailed articles by Leclercq, Jean: "*Ioculator et saltator*, S. Bernard et l'image du jongleur dans les manuscrits", in *Translatio Studii*, ed. J. Plante, Collegeville, St. John's Univ. Press, 1973, and Ogilvy, J. D. A.: "*Mimi, scurrae, histriones*" in *Speculum*, 38.4, October 1963, pp. 603-619. Both give a valuable résumé of the medieval testimonia, but do not attempt to assess the *scurra*'s specific role.

For the Roman *Iuventus*, see: Eyben, E.: *De jonge Romein*, Brussels, Paleis der Academiën, 1977, especially pp. 161-167 on Youth and the Theatre; also Morel, Jean-Paul: "La *Iuventus* et les Origines du Théâtre Romain", in *Rev. des Etudes Latines*, 1969, pp. 208-252. Morel does not deal with the *Iuventus* of Plautus and misses the *scurra* altogether.

Index Locorum

Acta Sanctorum ed. J. Bollandus
VII (752B) 83
AGOBERT
Lib. de disp. rer. eccles.
(= MGH, Ep.V.S. 178) 78
APULEIUS
Metam. 1 (4) 55
ARTEMIDORUS
Oneirocrit. 1 (78) 16
ATHENAEUS
Deipnosoph. 6 (235f-236e, f)
6; (238e) 18; (239f-246b) 5
AUCTORIS INCERTI
Carm. de Philom. (25) 66
Biblia Sacra (*Versio Vulg.*)
II *Reg.* (6.20) 82
CATULLUS
Carm. (22.12) 65
CICERO
Quinct. (11), (55), (62) 60
Verr. 2 (3.146) 59
Cluent. (39) 59
Mur. (13) 61
Cat. 2 (4.7) 72
De Harusp. Resp. (42) 28, 59,
79
Sest. (39) 28, 59
Cael. (27) 55
ad Att. 6 (3.5) 2
ad Fam. 9 (21.3) 59
de Rep. 2 (22.40) 28

de Nat. Deor. 1 (93) 3
Orat. (26.90) 60
Corp. Gloss. Lat.
II (180, 592) 2
IV (390) 2
V (243, 610, 614) 2
Corp. Inscr. Lat.
VI (1063) 53
DIOMEDES
Ars Gramm. III (= Keil,
Gramm. Lat. I, 490) 67
GELLIUS
16 (10.15) 28
Historia Augusta
Verus (8.11) 72
Comm. (1.7-8) 72
Elagab. (33.7) 37, 73
Sev. Alex. (61) 37, 74
Sept. Sev. (22.4-5) 73
Maxim. Duo (9.4) 74
Tyr. XXX (33) 75, 76
Aurel. (42.5) 76
Gall. (9.5), (17.7), (21.6) 75;
(21.6) 79
HORACE
Serm. 1 (1.102) 69; 1 (4.81-
85) 62, 81; 1 (5.56-69) 66;
1 (8.11), 2 (1.22) 68; 2
(3.175, 224) 69
Epist. 1 (15) 80
Ars Poet. (225) 3

You will never forget that true and radiant morn
when in those happy surroundings you were gathered
beneath the shade of the tree of life
planted in what was paradise.

That same tree of life still exists in memories
as the tree grows from earth to heaven
and your tears will nourish its growth
while the sun still bursts brightly still.

In memory of all our children

My eyes can no longer see your smile
yet my heart still feels its warmth.
My ears can no longer hear your voice
yet your words of wisdom are etched into every day.
I can no longer hold your hand
yet it still guides my every step.
What we see, hear, touch is only temporary
but what we feel, learn and love is eternal.
You are always with me.

Contents

FOREWORD

What is a legacy? That was not a question asked when I had the germ of an idea for this book when listening to a broadcast of "You and Yours" on Radio 4 some time ago discussing organ transplants. It included interviews with parents whose child's organs had been donated to save the lives of other people and I thought at that time "what greater legacy can there be?"

Since then, though, I have learned there are numerous colours to the term legacy, not just in my own life but in the many people I have been privileged to "meet" on the road to this publication.

There are several definitions you can find in dictionaries as well as that mentioned later in this book and the following are some, I feel, encapsulate the essence of the meaningful legacies you will read about:

"Something that is left behind after a person has passed away"

"Legacy of sharing what you have learned, not just earned"

"Bequeathing values over valuables"

"A person's legacy is known not from the number of years lived but the life lived"

And how pertinent is that last definition when we connect it with the loss of a beloved child which this book is predominantly about.

But there is another reason that prompted me toward this project, that of sparse literature available that focused on a legacy which ultimately, I contend, is a positive outcome of a tragic event. I have read several books and countless articles on the subject of the death of a loved one but rarely do they touch on a legacy. Not that such stories are not profoundly readable with the pathway from initial loss littered with all the myriad emotions connected to grief; anguish, denial, anger, guilt and many, many more.

You might wonder whether a legacy is created by the person who has died or the person left behind. I don't believe I can honestly answer that question. What I do know is that in such profound loss of a child those left behind are fundamentally changed. Their values and outlook on life undergo an upheaval of their inner self that invariably will have a far reaching effect on not only themselves but those immediately around them.

Three legacies that have received widespread publicity in this country have had the profound effect of changing British law; that of Helen's Law, Sarah's Law and what might be termed Harry's law. The first resulted in murderers who do not reveal the whereabouts of their victim will not be

1

considered for parole and the second a disclosure scheme to find out where sex offenders are. The third and most recent was a change of immunity from prosecution law for diplomats and their families. What brave and determined mothers who pursued these changes I am sure leaves us all humble.

You will find an amazing variety of legacies depicted in the book which are equally so valuable to society at large but often go unsung. They are remarkable for their diversity and profoundness in equal measure but more importantly, no matter how big or small, have a common thread running through them and that thread is love.

Tears may very well accompany the reading of the lives of children cut short so tragically but through those tears the legacies shine a bright glimmer of light through the sorrowful clouds.

As this book has been well over a year in the making certain events and predictions into the following year may not be entirely accurate, particularly in view of the onset of the pandemic that has changed so many lives in this year of publication.

You, the reader, might also wonder why I have delved into the subject in such depth so I guess before the many stories in this book unfold in each poignant page I should tell you about my own son's story.

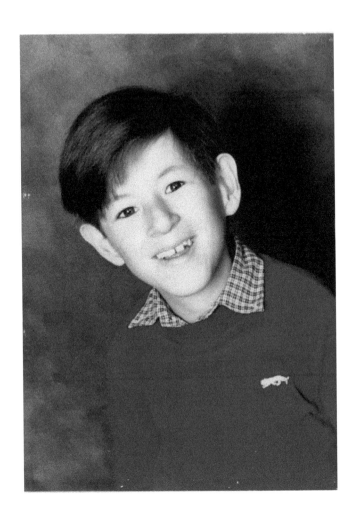

ANDREW BAGLEY
2.1.1973 to 10.9.1988

My wife and I had waited so long for our first and what would be our only child so the joy of his birth could not be described. His thick dark hair showed more emphasis of genes from my wife than myself, already rapidly receding.

A healthy weight belied problems that arose after just a few days as epicanthic folds of his eyes and "clicky" hips were diagnosed. Whilst the eyes were quickly resolved the hips necessitated us going straight from the maternity to general hospital where our new son Andrew was put in plaster to prevent his hip dislocating. Just over a year later when we thought this initial worry was resolving and we could get on with enjoying his babyhood we were shocked to learn he would need a plate inserted by operation to prevent complete dislocation.

Shock was soon replaced by determination to see it through but his post-operative recovery resulted in the onset of epilepsy, perhaps due to the brightly lit recovery room he was placed in. This additional worry would take some four years to resolve into petit mal seizures managed fairly effectively with a balanced medication.

As first-time parents, with no comparison to make, we began to be concerned about his progress after his second birthday so the next shock to our system was to be informed the likelihood he would never progress mentally beyond young childhood. Only the first of two occasions, I cried not just for Andrew but our own expectations of his future and our part in them.

As he approached four he was getting more vocal though not fluent in speech and his mobility had not quite reached walking stage when he started at a special needs school. The care and devotion of the staff could not be faulted and so a long association began with the staff, many of its pupils and later going on the board of governors.

Andrew was becoming an endearing character as his speech developed further, comically using the third person to describe himself and I recall one particularly funny event when he approached a teacher, Janet, having a very busy time: "Oh Andrew! Shall we run away from all this and enjoy ourselves?" to which Andrew replied "can we have our dinner first"!

Home life continued, my wife, who was an excellent mother, caring for Andrew whilst I worked and when I was home I took over most of his care, entering his childhood world with games and drawings, the latter of which would become a feature later on with murals on his bedroom wall and one even painted with many cartoon characters at the local children's A&E.

The next worry came soon after his sixth birthday when he was diagnosed with scoliosis which may have been at least partly prompted by the hip operation which had slightly shortened his left leg and therefore caused an uneven gait when he eventually started walking at five though what a joy that was at the time.

The spinal curve meant he had to wear a body jacket that wrapped around his torso and reached just below his hips and supported his chin at the top. It took some getting used to as he had to wear it all day but Andrew accepted it so readily his resilience was remarkable. Apart from applying surgical spirits to areas that became sore and refitting every 18 months we got on with life and his enjoyment in it.

He loved school, being one of a few who spoke quite well resulting in him associating more with the teachers than his fellow pupils and enjoyed the trips I arranged for them to London at Christmas and zoos and theme parks in the summer thanks to a Mencap mini bus.

The next hurdle was a heart operation to close a hole in his heart that should have closed at birth. This was considered particularly necessary as it was envisaged he would need to be in good health for major surgery on his back later. With transfer to Great Ormond Street due to his multiple problems the heart operation went really well and he bounced back to full health in little more than a month.

Life rolled on as Andrew further developed to about a mental age of three by the time he reached nine and his most enthusiastic places to visit were zoos and with pastimes including countless puzzles and favourite TV shows such as Masters of the Universe and Muppets this settled period was enjoyed to the full.

The next and what would be the final hill to climb was his back operation at the end of 1982. It was decided to carry this out earlier than was desired due to further growth to come for the spine because the curve was increasing more severely. The first two weeks in hospital found him on a striker bed which entailed steel bars attached through his ankles and head with weights at each end in order to obtain the maximum stretching of his spine before fusion with two steel bars adhered to the spine with wires.

The difficulty of the striker bed cannot be overstated and was the only occasion he resisted treatment in his short life. The operation, which took a grueling ten hours resulted in over five months of recovery, three in intensive care where leafless trees turned to blossom, during which he nearly died three times. The joy of coming out of a long coma by clutching his little Paddington bear is a memory that remains with me forever.

Andrew slowly progressed over the summer of 1983 and returned to his beloved school that autumn and for us it seemed a return to relative normality. Countless memories flood back of holidays playing in the sand or donning elfin hats in magical woodlands and of course zoos where his favourite animal, albeit not too close, was the elephant.

It was about this time when Andrew's beloved pet rabbit died and it was not easy to explain to him about death. We decided to bury him in the garden and offered up a solemn prayer for God to look after him in his rabbit heaven. However, we remained speechless when Andrew, who clearly hadn't understood the concept of death, uttered the words "dig him up again Dad"!

My wife enjoyed dressing him in lovely clothes, influenced occasionally by t-shirts and jumpers depicting elephants, Muppets, Mr Men and such like matching his pyjamas and bed linen. We also took the opportunity of a summer play-scheme arranged by Great Ormond Street at Tadworth, Surrey enabling us to have yearly holidays to ourselves and re-charge our emotional batteries.

But this seemingly settled period gradually came to an end as the spinal operation failed to hold the curve resulting in his mobility declining. I often thought at this time that the decision not to return to the jacket regime, whilst relieving, was surprising but among several medical decisions we questioned, it was fruitless to dwell on this and so we again adapted to his declining health condition.

By his fifteenth birthday he was enjoying his limited life, by now in a wheelchair for distances, including weekly visits to the local children's A&E when he would "advise" me which characters to depict on the mural from Jungle Book, Snow White and the Seven Dwarfs and many more Disney favourites. We decided it would be good for all three of us for Andrew to return to Tadworth that summer which he enjoyed so much and we booked a holiday in Interlaken.

However, three days into the holiday we were phoned to be advised Andrew had developed a chest infection and would be taken to the adjoining hospital but only as a precaution. We agonised over returning immediately but were reassured it was not necessary as he might return to the play-scheme in a couple of days.

However, after regular contacts over the next two days his condition declined and with transfer to Great Ormond Street being arranged we took an emergency flight home and, with my brother and his wife there for us we looked down on a poorly Andrew.

A week passed before the fateful news was told to us that there was nothing more they could do for him and all we could do was take him home to die. For only the second time in his life I wept and my wife who I had supported so much throughout was the one to support me.

We took him home and because he had nearly died seven times in his short life there was still a glimmer of hope but fast fading as oxygen was brought in for his final few days.

He died peacefully in a bed next to me after an out of character comment "had enough Dad" the day before and so it was over. The brightest of lights in my life had been extinguished and the darkness enveloped us. We mourned a loving child so loved as the blur of funeral and after effects took its toll that it was not until weeks later we began our first legacy for Andrew with a fund-raising dance in aid of Great Ormond Street.

I returned two months later to complete, amid sorrow and pride, my personal legacy to Andrew with the completion of the hospital mural. I believe it still remains with a plaque below commemorating Andrew and the National Association for Children in Hospital which I was a treasurer for.

The years rolled by with my continued involvement with Compassionate Friends but sadly my marriage ended and eventually ten years later I married another bereaved parent whose children died of undiagnosed cardiomyopathy.

But before that another opportunity for a legacy unexpectedly presented itself when, after joining a local drama group, I was asked if I would like to audition for a TV advert. I did but initially was unsuccessful. However, soon after a request was made for another advert, Lemsip, the audition for which I succeeded in.

The day for filming arrived when I found myself outside one of Andrew's favourite places, Whipsnade Zoo. How I hesitated and thought of the irony as I walked past the elephant enclosure feeling Andrew's spirit enveloping me.

My role as a zoo keeper took me to the chimpanzee enclosure where, dressed in a suitable uniform I had to pass by, do a double take as I saw a female keeper in the cage full of cold and say "You don't look well, you should be in bed" However, on the first take I mistakenly said "You don't look well, we should be in bed". CUT!

Several months after the filming I received a generous cheque and approached the zoo resulting in a bench being placed outside the elephants' enclosure with a plaque reading "In memory of Andrew, his love of elephants will live on". Although the enclosure was moved some time after so was the bench and I believe it is still there now.

There are still difficult times when grief, lying just below the surface of my consciousness, erupts with tears and an overwhelming sadness, prompted by some external agency such as someone asking if I have children. But then parents who do have other children have their own hill to climb as they put some of their own grief on hold to support them. Then of course there are parents, yes parents, of the unborn, snatched from the womb during the vagaries of pregnancy

However, I now close my story of Andrew in the hope of success for this publication in memory of his name and all the children contained in this book. The royalties will go jointly to Compassionate Friends and Cardiac Risk in the Young, the latter of which I have also supported with a book of children's stories in memory of my wife's children as too have their friends which has so far raised over £14,000.

JOSHUA TIMOTHY HALLAM
3.12.1991 to 19.2.2015

"You've a strong one here, Mrs. Hallam" were the words spoken by the doctor carrying out the routine health check the day after Josh was born. This statement proved to be true of Josh in so many ways.

Physically it had been demonstrated even before birth as Josh seemed determined to lie sideways in the womb, managing to manoeuvre back to that position a number of times after doctors manipulated him round saying there was not enough room for him to do it again.

As a baby and young child he was content, happy, lively and outgoing. Even as a baby he would try to make eye contact with strangers and make them smile. His older brother Matthew and sister Victoria had been much more quiet and shy so it was like having a little whirlwind entering our household.

He was a very physically active and capable little boy who loved climbing anything; windowsills, our garden fence, garden gate. The worst example of this found him some way from the house happily chatting to a lady who'd been out riding her horse and spotted Josh on his own. On another occasion Josh had climbed to the top of the climbing frame at our local park and before I knew what was happening a chap had climbed up and brought him down admonishing me for having allowed Josh to climb at such a young age. Josh was not impressed!

Josh loved nursery and primary school. Not always the most compliant and biddable child (he always needed to see the reason for a rule), but always surrounded by friends, and having fun.

He was musical, playing cornet and piano and excelled at Taekwondo, a Korean martial art, which was a great outlet for his energy. Secondary education took him to an all-boys school where he worked really hard at the subjects he loved and got by in the ones he was less keen on. He did well enough in his GCSEs to begin a BTEC course in computing at 6th form college. This was definitely his area of expertise and he had a great start there.

He had a lovely group of friends, boys and girls with whom he spent much of his time. They went camping in the Lake District and to Leeds Music Festival a couple of times.... highlights of his life. One of his great joys was cinema, he really loved film and during his illness later on, this was the one activity he could still do and he made the most of that.

With hindsight, it is clear to see Josh was already unwell at the beginning of 6th form. He had lost a lot of weight but had purposely cut down on junk food so, to my shame, I missed a warning sign. He became increasingly tired and one evening said he had a swelling in his neck. Suddenly, putting all the changes together I somehow knew something was badly wrong. A visit to our GP the next evening resulted in us being sent directly to hospital. To cut a long story short he was diagnosed with Chronic Myeloid Leukaemia and treatment was to begin immediately.

Josh's first reaction was one of bewilderment really, saying he wasn't sure how he was supposed to feel. What he was sure about however was that he would do whatever doctors advised and have any treatment available to him. His Dad and I promised that whatever his treatment entailed he would never have to go through it alone.

Although very rare in someone just turned seventeen, the outlook was positive: an effective tablet treatment was successfully enabling a great many patients to live relatively normal lives with their cancer.

Because of his age, at the beginning of his treatment at our local hospital Josh was given the option of transferring to the Young Oncology Unit (supported by Teenage Cancer Trust) at the Christie Hospital in Manchester. This is a specialist unit for young people aged between 16-24 and strangely enough I vividly remembered walking past the entrance to this unit when my Mum was receiving radiation treatment in the Christie a couple of years previously. I can remember how terrible I thought it was that there was a need for such a place.

Josh declined to have his treatment at the Christie, being quite content with the consultant specialists in Preston and not feeling the need, as he put it to make any "cancer friends". It was his intention to have his treatment and carry on his life as normally as possible. We did however go to the Christie, sent by our consultant for second opinion and advice.

Also at this time, as a backup plan for worst case scenario Josh's brother and sister were tested there for bone marrow compatibility. Back home Josh was trying to carry on at college whilst going for blood tests and result appointments every few days.

Unfortunately the drug was proving ineffective in Josh's case probably because his disease had been more advanced than first thought at the time of diagnosis. His treatment was supplemented with blood and platelet transfusions but he had become very poorly. There was no choice other than to be transferred to the Christie where the greatest expertise was to be found.

On Friday 3rd April 2009 we attended the Christie. Josh was told how very poorly he was by one of the consultants and that he would need to be admitted. There was one more drug which could be tried before the final option of a bone marrow transplant - which would come from Josh's sister as thankfully, she was as good a match as was possible.

This was the point where our lives really changed. Josh accepted his studies would have to be suspended. In going to the Christie we had really entered the world of cancer.

One of the wonderful things about the Christie unit was that parents or others could stay. As well as having a pull down bed in Josh's room, just down the corridor was a little "home" set up, comprising lounge, kitchen and six bedrooms.

Whenever Josh was in hospital I stayed there and met the most wonderful young people and their parents, all mutually supportive of each other, and our children. In this place I met the bravest of the brave.

Apart from one or two days at home Josh's first admission lasted five and a half months, much of this time in isolation, and during which time he was twice admitted to Critical Care. Treatment was unsuccessful and he did need the transplant. Conditioning for a transplant is intensely grueling with the patient receiving intense chemotherapy and total body irradiation to kill their own bone marrow and with it, their immune system. Isolation and hygiene protocols before a transplant are strictly adhered to.

As mentioned, his Leeds Festival experiences were the highlights of his young life and he was very attached to his wristbands which he never removed. Such was Josh's charm he managed to persuade his consultant he should be allowed to keep them on, albeit very thoroughly cleaned and disinfected.

As far as we could tell initially the transplant had gone well, but for any patient this is just the start. So many things went wrong for Josh. He developed severe graft versus host disease which affected his liver. He became suddenly allergic to the anti-rejection drug resulting in epileptic fits which necessitated a transfer to another hospital, unconscious and ventilated. On this occasion he woke up in intensive care on his eighteenth birthday, he was allowed one birthday balloon by his bed!

He had to take massive doses of steroids and suffered severe side effects: massive weight gain, Diabetes, cataracts, Avascular Necrosis in hips and knees resulting in him being dependent on a wheelchair. He was very susceptible to infection, often chest infections, and would often need intravenous antibiotics. The source of the infections were not always identifiable and unfortunately one of the places infection had found a home was in Josh's heart. By the time it was found it had done major damage.

After having been told very brutally after a heart scan at another hospital that no surgeon would consider operating on such a high risk patient he returned to the Christie and immediately began researching relevant operations and emailing hospitals he thought might be able to help.

This was Josh, strong and determined, exploring all avenues with a tremendous will to live. A little later, stuck in a wheelchair and needing a hip replacement (the first of four joints which would need replacing) he was telling his consultant, in yet another hospital, that despite the terrible pain he constantly suffered, he loved his life. What people remember about him is his bravery, compassion, kindness, sense of fun and all things ridiculous.

Josh's aim was always to resume studying and determined as ever he found a way back in, eventually studying for and achieving a foundation degree in computing. His lecturers were so supportive, completely understanding his limitations but also how much he wanted to succeed.

He was once again in hospital when he learned he had graduated. He had also passed his driving test, thoroughly enjoying the freedom this gave him. He loved his car. It was very difficult to get a team together to perform the hip operation with the heart and lung problems Josh had and by the time it took place he was much weaker than was ideal. Recovery proved very difficult and Josh, although determined, never regained his mobility.

He was in hospital for three of his birthdays. His twenty first party had to be cancelled and he finally had it one year later. There was so much he wanted to do but was unable: bungee jumping, snowboarding, travelling. He had a burning desire to attend the USA San Diego Comic-Con and managed to get tickets in 2014. Beside himself with excitement he set about planning the trip.

However, his condition worsening, the plans had to be abandoned. He was so disappointed and everyone felt his disappointment. He did manage a trip to New York later that year with oxygen in tow, thanks to his dad and sister who took him. On his return though and being unwell it was straight to hospital for another admission.

Josh passed away suddenly and unexpectedly, although he had been unwell, on 19th February 2015. It has been impossible to cover everything that happened. I would say that of the six years he was ill, if you were to total all the admissions at least two of those were spent in hospital.

For a boy who was reluctant to be admitted to the Christie he soon grew to love the place. His unit was brilliantly suited to patients of his age group going through the most terrifying time of their lives. This special place really understands young people and gives them space to be themselves. Josh made strong friendships here. Some friends recovered and some did not. Josh attended more funerals than someone of his age should need to.

Josh was utterly devoted to the Young Oncology Unit and was a very active and vocal member of its patient steering group, influencing what was provided for patients. He had strong views on the care young people should receive and wanted future patients to receive the same benefits he had.

It was this devotion which informed Josh's legacy. Within the wider Christie charity Josh has a named fund which feeds directly into the "Activities Fund" of the Young Oncology Unit. The fund pays for occasional trips and on-ward activities run by artists, musicians etc., activities which can provide a welcome change of focus from grueling rounds of testing and treatments. In the past five years friends and family have to date raised nearly £45k. This is such a special place where Josh felt loved, safe and secure and we know without a shadow of doubt he would approve.

Losing Josh has had the most devastating effect on us all: myself, Ian, Matthew, Victoria and wider family and friends. Josh had been close to death a number of times and as the Mum of one of his friend said when she heard he had died "but Josh always gets better".

We are bereft still. I quickly realised that we don't have the language to describe losing your child, the words simply do not exist. The magnitude of our loss is infinite. Having said that though, he is, we feel, still with us in everything we do. He is certainly with me always.

Shortly after Josh died the head teacher of our primary school contacted us and asked if we would put Josh's name to an award which would be given annually to a child leaving to move to high school. The Josh Hallam Memorial Award is given for "Outstanding kindness and friendship to others".

I feel frustrated that within this account I have not been able to describe fully just what a force of nature Josh was and how much potential was lost. He was the most caring and loving young man. I feel hugely privileged to have had him at all and blessed that we spent so much time together, even in really difficult circumstances.

Even when things were at their worst he was always kind and considerate, never taking his frustrations out on me or others around him. He loved treating people, buying gifts was such a joy for him and it's fitting that gifting continues in his name.

AIDAN O'NEILL
18.3.1998 to 29.9.2010

On the 18th March 1998 following a completely uneventful pregnancy and a very speedy labour - we only just made it to the maternity hospital - Aidan quietly and without fuss joined his half brother and three half sisters in this world.

He was a very quiet and contented baby just as long as he was fed regularly, for a half hour every hour or so. His appetite never abated throughout his life. Food was always very important to him. Food was an adventure. Food was a never ending stream of new and exciting experiences.The words, "I don't like", did not exist in his vocabulary when it came to food.

He grew big and strong. He grew confident and comfortable with himself. He was very self-assured. Above all he showed enormous empathy for everything and everybody great and small. It was astonishing to see such empathy in someone so young. I believe it was because he was so comfortable with himself. He was incredibly gentle. He was unconventionally brave.

He would do mad things that most boys wouldn't countenance for fear of being bullied. For school he dressed up as the fairy on top of the christmas tree once complete with Tutu, fairy wings, magic wand, star and christmas tree shoved up his bottom. Everyone thought it was brilliant!

When he entered a room the sunshine came with him. He was universally loved. He could speak with children of childish things and adults with intelligence and interest.

This is Aidan: One day at school he noticed an injured Woodlouse. He picked it up and was showing it to a friend when another boy knocked it out of his hands and stamped on it. Aidan thumped him and the boy, the protagonist, went and told teacher. We were called to school over the incident. Aidan was duly admonished but said, if the same thing occurred again he would still thump the boy and take his punishment. The deputy head had a smile he struggled to contain. Afterwards he told us the boy in question was a nasty piece of work and whilst he couldn't condone Aidan's behaviour he thoroughly understood where he was coming from; it is a good trait to stick up for those who can't stick up for themselves.

After Aidan died it became apparent that he was always sensitive to other people's problems and issues whether that be with some homework or other more important things. It seems he was a kind friend, an understanding ear and a good laugh.

Although he excelled at school it transpired he was the school joker. Always up for a laugh; a practical joke; a witty remark. He was like this at home but we didn't consider that he'd continue this way at school.

He was also habitually honest. He understood that when he did wrong he was always better off if he could own up to it before anyone else could drop him in it. He somehow worked out early in life that coming clean with humility and sorrow were absolutely guaranteed to deflate anybody's anger.

During the summer of 2006 Aidan's aunt, who had been in Tanzania helping with a project there to build a new secondary school and bring fresh water to the village of Mtitu, sponsored an 18 year old Tanzanian student to come to the UK. Aidan took to her immediately. He wanted to learn all about Shangwe's life and the life of young people in Tanzania. He wanted to know about how they lived, what they ate, what school was like.They became great friends.

Inspired, the following year we were able to go on holiday to Tanzania. We went on safaris. We saw Elephants, Lions, Leopards... It was fantastic. But that wasn't the highlight for Aidan. We spent some time in the Mufindi Highlands where we had the privilege to visit and meet some people from a small village. Like many villages in east Africa the villagers had nothing that western boys would recognise. Plastic bags balled up with string for footballs, bare feet, bicycle tyres and a stick to play with. It felt like the whole of humanity lived outside in the mud. But what struck Aidan most of all was how happy they were. It affected him profoundly. He said, "I feel ashamed Dad. We have everything. Computers, game boys, a nice house, cars and we're on holiday and we often moan about this and that and we say we're bored and yet here are these children who have none of our "things" and yet they are among the happiest people I have ever met. They're the most generous too as they'll share with us what little they have". This was a big deal for a nine year old and I couldn't have been more proud of him.

We met up with Shangwe and her uncle Tito in Dar Es Salaam for a lovely evening meal on the last night of our holiday. Tito is an inspirational man. It was he who'd come up with the plan for a school in his village. Aidan spent the entire evening talking to Tito, learning what compelled him to build a school, to get fresh water for his village. What motivated him to keep going year after year to realise his dream. And this is what Aidan learnt.

Tito understood that the people of his village were getting ill because of contaminated water so he wanted to build a well and pumps to deliver clean fresh water to the village. But the people of the village thought he was crazy. Everyone knew you got ill because of evil spirits and curses. You could see the water was clean, besides they'd been drinking it for years. Everyone just said there was no need and besides he could never build it.

"So why", asked Aidan, "are you building a school?".

State education is only provided up to age 11 in Tanzania. Many Africans believe their way out of poverty is through education. So it was that Shangwe had to travel two days away from her village for expensive secondary education. Tito wanted to provide free secondary schooling in his village for three reasons he told Aidan. One; so that the villagers could get a proper secondary education without having to leave their village. Two; part of what they'd learn in secondary school is that invisible organisms live in the water that otherwise looks clean and that these organisms are a major cause of disease. Three; everybody said he couldn't build a school.

Tito reasoned that if he could build a school it would shut up everybody who said he couldn't do it. He'd have a growing body of people who demanded clean water. And his people would be on their way to higher education and could climb their way out of poverty. On our return from Tanzania Aidan started to raise money for Tito and his village to help build a school and bring fresh water to the village. We helped by putting on charity shows to raise some money too.

On September 29th 2010, just a few days after starting grammar school, Aidan fell off of his bike on his way to school. He ruptured his liver and died in hospital an hour or so later.

Friends of ours, to celebrate Aidan's life, wanted to put on a show for us in his memory. There was no way either of us could sit through that show without becoming gibbering wrecks sobbing on the floor so we said we would join in the show and we would make it about Aidan and his passion for Tanzania. And in this kind act, Aidan's Angels was formed.

Over the years we have raised many thousands of pounds for Tito and Mtitu. Because all of the money goes directly to the Mtitu Foundation there is no government corruption to siphon any off. It all goes directly to the project, to school buildings and staff. The village has several wells, pumps and clean water.

In 2012 Tito invited us to stay with him in the village to open the first completed school block, Aidan's Block. Aidan's brother Alex stayed on in Mtitu for three months when he commenced building of the second block that has become Alex's block.

Although Aidan never got to see Mtitu it was very strange that while we were there for a few days to open the block his presence could be felt all around us more profoundly than at any other time since he left us. It's as if he has found his spiritual home there and is looking after them as he looked after children in his own school when he was little.

MEGAN CLARKSON
27.1.2016 TO 2.1.2019

I have a very vivid memory of the time when I knew that Megan would continue somehow after she died and whilst I am not sure if the events of my memory are real, the time, the place etc., the feelings very much are. Some of what I am about to write is felt by every parent, but not every parent sets up a Legacy. The way you feel about your child is very personal, you know them like no other and you feel for them like no other. Grief to me is a word that has lost its meaning; it's not a process, it's a show of love and whilst my love for Megan is unique so is my grief. My reasons for Megan's Journey, for sharing my daughter with the world are incredibly selfish. This is not for her, it's for me.

Megan, my beautiful whirlwind of a daughter died at 00:09 on 2nd January 2019. She would be 3 that very same January. I remember always looking at Megan and just being in awe of the sassy little girl I had created; that I was helping to mould. Her take no prisoner/take no bullshit attitude was exactly what I wanted her to have. At 2 years old she knew her own mind and wasn't scared to say it. I would look on with pride and admiration.

As a 37-year-old woman I did not have that sense of self that my 2-year-old did, and I would hope she would never lose it. I would fight for her to keep that. 16 months on from her death I am still paralysed by the pain of losing this. Not just the presence of Megan but the notion of who she would be and what she would do. I will forever be haunted by the loss of what my intelligent, thoughtful and fearless daughter would bring to the world.

Megan belonged in this world, she owned it in a way I will never. I go through my life watching and taking part, but Megan was life itself, she captivated you in a way that is just indescribable. I know this is felt by all parents, but we have had strangers tell us this, she just had a sparkle to her. At 00:09, 2nd January, a doctor looked at me through pain and sorrow and told me that which I called her in for, to tell me that life itself was over.

The hours that passed went by in a blur of holding Megan and thinking into the abyss. Thinking of a time that every parent does not let their minds wander to, outliving their children. And my memory, how real the facts are I do not know, is this. Looking at a clock that said 02:20 and I remember vividly thinking that this is a time that does not know Megan. Not that Megan does not know this time, but time itself does not know her. The thought of that still tears my heart apart over and over again but in the rawness of my immediate loss the pain of the thinking that the world around me would not know my Megan was just unbearable.

I vowed to myself at that time that the world and time would know Megan and they will know exactly who my incredible daughter was and what she would become. They would know she was so desperate to be older; she would try so many things when she reached that elusive age of 3. God how I want her to be able to try them. On her next birthday she would be 5, the age she saw her older brother brush his teeth independently and being the independent little lady that she was, she could not wait for this. They would see how caring she was, at 2 years old feeling the emotion of everything and really understanding it, the colour fading from Princess Poppy in Trolls causing Megan to sob for her sadness.

I vowed in that second, not for Megan but for the world and selfishly for myself. The world was gone to Megan, I don't get the comfort of the afterlife that I have no belief in. Megan feels no more, and she is no more, no matter how much I wish it was different. As truly awful as that sounds it is my truth but that does not mean that Megan is gone from the world, she continues in the stories I tell and the legacy I create for her.

As much as I would love to say I am a humanitarian, that I do this solely to do good it would be a half truth. Yes, I want to help those who helped my family, all the money in the world can never repay the kindness shown to us. Yes, I want to show the world how a mother grieves her child and its ok, not something to be fearful of. But above all that I have to keep my daughter within the present because although she is not physically here, and my heart is broken beyond repair by this, my sanity would shatter if the persona of Megan could not be felt by everyone around me and everyone I am yet to meet.

Megan's Journey began as a blog whilst Megan was in hospital fighting for her life against Pleuropulmonary Blastoma, a rare lung cancer found in children. It was created to keep our friends and family in the loop regarding Megan's treatment and progress. 3 days after its creation, 21 days after hearing the words "there is a lump", Megan left this world and me. At this point it changed, it became an outpouring for my grief and the response to this has been comforting.

I have had other grieving parents tell me I put into words the pain that they feel that they want others to see and understand. I have had friends and family tell me it helps them understand me and my post-apocalyptic life. We also fundraise for a charity or a cause that helps each of the 3 hospitals Megan received care in. We fundraise for Ronald McDonald House, Glasgow who provided us with a roof over our heads as our daughter's journey ended in Royal Hospital for Children, Glasgow and for the play staff at The Children's Ward, The Victoria Hospital Kirkcaldy, our local hospital where the play staff keep children entertained and help them through some difficult times. And for LoveOliver, a childhood cancer charity who provide so much practical support to all families across Scotland fighting childhood cancer.

I also fight for earlier diagnosis for rare cancers in children. No doctor let Megan down, the system lets down the doctors and nurses. Not just for the child fighting cancer but for the child undiagnosed by a stroke, by a rare metabolic condition. The support and kindness shown to my family through Megan's diagnosis will never leave me, neither will the fight I had to put up, to get primary healthcare to progress her and that it was not just a cough, not simply viral as we parents of young children hear so many times. I do not want any parent to have to fight like I did or to suffer unnecessarily, as my Megan had to.

Since Megan's death 16 months ago, over £27,000 has been raised in her memory, doctors have made small, but helpful changes to how they treat children with coughs, so whilst the reasons for Megan's legacy come from a mother's need to have her child in the present, the good this can bring is apparent. I know my caring daughter would be happy to see people who need help receive it. The passion and zest for life Megan had would change the world, as her mother it's now my job to do this for her, and in the words of my forever 2-year-old... I'll do my best!

DILLY OVINGTON
31.10.1971 to 12.2.1999

I came home with Dilly, after 48hrs in hospital, in an ambulance from Cheltenham, as my mother was looking after my son, Ben for me while I was away. She always found it really funny, to see me skipping up the garden path in my nighty and slippers, holding my 2 day old daughter, totally forgetting I had just given birth!!!! And that was the beginning of 26yrs of the life of Dilly.

Why Dilly? Well her name was Catherine, but her brother could not get his tongue round this name, at 19months, and the name Dilly evolved. She hated it until she went to her secondary school, and the head girl was called Dilly, so suddenly, it was very ok!

From a very young age, she loved to sing. She sang all the way to school each morning, and once, going to Cornwall on holiday, she asked my husband and I if we would like to hear some songs from her new "Singing together" book. We obviously said yes, and she took a big breath, and sang all the way to Cornwall!!!!

Dilly was always full of fun, scatty, lovable, and adored her brother. She was also lucky enough to have 12 cousins, who she was very close to. She was a great one for organising plays for us to watch, and songs for us to listen to. Slightly bossy I think!!

She also loved and excelled at many sports. She learnt to swim at a very early age, and I remember her frightening lifeguards at a public pool as she jumped in the deep end aged 3, and they jumped in to save her, and were most unpopular with her as she fought them off!! She rode beautifully, and loved her ponies, graduating to horses, and competed very successfully in Pony Club competitions and local events. She was often caught singing on her ponies as she exercised them, lighting up the life of ramblers she met on the way. She played tennis well, competing in many tournaments, and was a team hockey player at school.

She was a weekly boarder at her secondary school, and it was here that her music really got going. Her music teacher suggested she started playing the tuba, as this would help and strengthen her lungs for singing, and she played in the school orchestra. A wonderful instrument that took up most of the back of my car each weekend! She made many good friends at this school, but she then went to Cheltenham Boys College for the sixth form, as they had just started taking girls, and her brother was there. This was when Dilly's true character really took off. She auditioned for Cabaret during the summer holidays, before she even started at the school in September, and got the lead part!! The Lisa Minelli of Cheltenham. How she loved those fish net tights!! So her first term was all about rehearsals and performing at Cheltenham's theatre, The Everyman, for 4 days and nights, where she sung her heart out and was such a star. We were so proud of her.

Cheltenham College have a wonderful chapel and the choir was, and still is, fabulous. She joined a few girls who sung in what was basically an all-boys choir. For her 2 years in the sixth form, she sung in the choir every Sunday, in all concerts, and sung many solo parts. Her voice was so powerful, you could always hear her distinctly above everyone else. On her final day of school she did a wonderful solo, "I waited for the Lord", Mendelssohn, which took our breath away, and brought me to tears. Very fortunately, one of her friends recorded it on an ancient ghetto blaster, and to this day it is my most treasured memory.

She had a gap year of travelling round the world, which went by in the usual chaotic, happy way that Dilly's life took. We baled her out of various incidents along the way, but she came home a little wiser, very happy, and her wonderful entertaining self. Our house became alive again, with her laughter, and hugs.

My son got married that summer, and Dilly sung a beautiful solo in the church at his wedding, which thankfully I have recorded too. To be able to still hear her voice is more than special.

She then announced that she wasn't ready to be sensible and settle down to a job, and decided to go to Val D'Isere for a season to work. She fell in love with the life, the skiing, and with an Australian snowboarder, Gumby, so she did a second season, with the intention of then returning to university after, for one year. But she returned in the summer and said she wanted to go back for just one more season. Her skiing had become excellent, and she was going to be given the chance to ski for England, so off she went.

I will always remember the last time I saw her, getting into her father's car to go to the airport. She was laughing, dropping things and generally being Dilly, and off they went. That vision haunts me to this day. If only I had known what was going to happen, if only I had hugged her harder, gone with her to the airport. Life is full of "if only's"now.

On February 12th, 1999, my life changed forever. I got home from work, and my son rang me from London. He started by saying I needed to sit down. He is a dreadful joker, and I said "ha ha Ben, stop joking." He then told me Gumby had rung him to say Dilly had been caught in an avalanche and died that morning, along with an Australian boy. Four others had escaped. My legs went to jelly, and my son said he was on his way. My husband and I had separated a year before this, so I was on my own, but the small Cotswold village I lived in were brilliant, even fighting off reporters who had somehow got hold of the story and were banging on my door, and fiercely removed by kind friends.

The following two weeks up to the funeral went by in a total blur, with snowboarding friends travelling from Val D'Isere, and arriving on my doorstep with nowhere to stay. A cottage in the village immediately was offered to us.

The funeral was beautiful, and that was that, all twenty years ago last Feb. I went through two years of really not being myself at all. I thought I was fooling everyone, but sadly, I was only fooling myself. My life had changed so much. I was divorced and on my own, and I had left a very large family, and was now down to my lovely son and my 2 beautiful granddaughters. I watched Dilly's friends get married, have children, and have good jobs. My friends were now serious grandparents, busy with their grandchildren, and of course I did as much as I could for my two, but you can't help thinking that Dilly would have been a wonderful mother as she adored children. I know her brother would have loved his daughters to know Dilly-she was such fun and made a huge impression on all children she met.

The years went by, and I became increasingly aware that I had never done anything in Dilly's memory. It's hard when you are on your own. Dilly and I used to sing together all the time, and so I joined a wonderful community choir in Cheltenham, and began to enjoy music again. A little idea niggled away in my head. What about a concert in her memory in Cheltenham College Chapel? I contacted her College tutor, Chris Haslam, and he loved the idea, and without his help and enthusiasm, I would never have dared do it. After much planning and huge help from the school, our choir sung in that wonderful place where I had heard Dilly singing for two years.

The college choir sang too - oh so beautiful. The head of music from the time when Dilly was there came and spoke about her, even reminding us that she was ALWAYS 10 minutes late for practice, but the wait was more than worth it!!!

Her tutor, Chris Haslam, spoke too, so proudly of her. He was Head of Drama and responsible for Dilly's success in Cabaret. The chapel was full, the atmosphere very special.

So Dilly goes on in the music world she loved. I was never sure if singing there would be too much for me, but it was wonderful. My beautiful, talented daughter SO deserved this. As everyone filed out of this beautiful chapel, we played the recording of her singing "I waited for the Lord" at her final speech day, and to hear her voice again, in that place was very moving.

I felt so much better after this. I felt at peace that I had done something to remember Dilly as she deserved. The £2000 we raised would be helping children to love music as she had. It was donated to the Gloucester Academy of Music, to provide music lessons to children who otherwise have no music education. She would have loved that.

The cup in her memory is given every year to the musician of the year at college, so her memory goes on in the wonderful music department of Cheltenham College.

Writing this is very apt, as it is 20yrs since she died, and me, my ex, and my son are going to Val D'Isere in the summer to see her memorial which we have never seen. A metal daffodil made by all her friends has been placed where she died. I shall take the recording of her beautiful voice, and listen to it in the mountains, in that very spot.

Thank you Dilly for making me a very proud mother. You are in my heart until we meet again.

Dilly remembered

A poem written by my sister on the 20th anniversary of her death.

She enters my head most days as a breath of snowy air, swooshing in
   and out of my thoughts.
Her laugh, her hair, her eyes, flashing like precious stones.
She's a baby, sitting smiling on a wooden chair.
She's a young child, riding a round pony.
She's a teenager, lying on the floor. She's a young woman, singing on a
   stage.
The thing is--------

She lives on in our heads never forgotten, always present
Forever full of life. Old age and wrinkles will never spoil her.
Mirrors won't reflect a face, saddened by years.
She'll be here always, full of energy and love. She was who she wanted
   to be.
She did what she wanted to do. She didn't pretend to be who she wasn't.
She taught us all a lesson that we should learn to live by,
Life is beautiful and can be gone in a millisecond. Life is...for
   being...you.
She meant so much to us all...We just didn't realise how much....

Until she was gone.
Don't look back and regret, look up at the sky and dream.
See colours, turn your face to the sun.
Watch the daffodils dancing in the warm spring breeze and.....
Think of her.

And from one of Dilly's best friends while waiting for her boys after school

And yet she seems so vibrant still. How cruel is fate?
Such sadness must consume always to know she's gone.
To birth and grow and care and love; this shining, sparkling, beautiful dove.
Sent just for you but "gone away", 21 years on this aching day.
No reason was that precious bud was picked, no wicked act or sins be licked.
Just that it was and so it is, for her to die and you to live.
What must you feel in all your hours, the loss, the lack of what could be?
The mother, sister, daughter, friend who will forevermore be young and free.
To sing and dance and love and be your shining, sparkling Daffo Dilly.

A very meaningful update

In July 2019, Dilly's father, brother Ben and I travelled to Val D'Isere, to see, at last, Dilly's stainless steel daffodil memorial in the mountains where she died. I had wanted to do this for so long, and was full of joy and nerves as we travelled out there. Also going were the Thorburns, who lost their son in the same avalanche, and had travelled from Australia, so we could all be together on this journey.

I had never been to Val D'Isere, so it was so strange to be in the place that Dilly loved so much. Gumby, Dilly's boyfriend at the time, met us on Saturday, to guide us up the mountain to the daffodil, which we would never have found without him. The walk was long and strenuous, and the scenery spectacular. The weather was hot and sunny, which was so lucky, as thunderstorms had been predicted, and if that had happened, the walk would not have taken place.

The last part of the walk was particularly steep and we were climbing through the forest over fallen trees, presumably knocked down by the avalanche. Suddenly, after 4 hours walking, Ben called out, "I can see it" and there it was, perched on the side of the mountain, beautiful in the sunlight. My dream for 20yrs, to see this wonderful memorial to my daughter Dilly.

We sat for a long time there, silent with our own memories, gazing at a view so breathtaking, Dilly's last view on earth. I had wanted to leave something there and had taken her Liberty print frog that had travelled the world with her, and had sat in my bedroom for 20years. Beneath the daffodil, was a little grotto, covered in ferns, and I placed him there, returning him to Dilly, in the perfect spot. We slowly dragged ourselves away, full of emotion, and the walk back down was done almost in silence, proud of ourselves for achieving such a marathon, and deep in thought.

We all had supper together. It was wonderful to catch up with Gumby again, who had been in the avalanche but survived, and I think for him too, this was a necessary and healing journey. It must have been difficult for him to take the parents to the very spot their children had died, and his beloved Dilly. But he did it with such grace, and looked after us so well. We couldn't have done it without his expertise and knowledge of the mountains.

All this was achieved in one weekend, as we all had to be home by Monday, and it wasn't until I was home, that I completely succumbed to nonstop tears and exhaustion. I knew it would bring all the raw details back to me, but I will never forget that weekend as being one of the most significant ones of my life, and I wouldn't have missed it for the world. I felt I had done right by Dilly, by visiting where she left us. As I sat by her beautiful daffodil I could hear, quite clearly, her magnificent voice singing to me, beautifully and clearly in the mountains. Love you Dilly, and thank you for the memories.

DANIEL REDMAN
2.10.1995 to 21.2.2016

Daniel was my third son, born a month after my fortieth birthday. A much wanted and planned-for baby who completed our family. He was a healthy, happy boy who quickly grew into a sturdy willful toddler with beautiful copper curls. When he was eighteen months old he experienced his first visit to A&E when he had managed to drink a whole bottle of Calpol despite the "childproof" cap. In the following years there were many more visits to hospital as Daniel grew into a fearless, risk-taking child and teenager.

Daniel's first love was football and one of my most enduring memories is of him as a toddler, running behind his two older brothers as they played football in our garden. Dan played in organised football from the age of four, in school teams and local Sunday league, eventually settling into the position of goalkeeper, playing for many different teams and collecting many trophies.

Daniel supported Burnley Football Club along with his brothers from a very early age. In later years he loved to travel to attend as many away games as possible; it was his aim to visit every football ground in the country and I have no doubt that he would have eventually fulfilled that dream. In reality he visited fifty of the ninety two current football league grounds. The walls of his bedroom are still covered with multiple football entrance tickets and train tickets.

The Saturday after his death Burnley Football Club paid tribute to him by putting Daniel's photograph on the huge screen in the twentieth minute of a local derby between Burnley and Blackburn and both sets of fans stood to applaud for a full minute. It was very moving but also unbelievably painful to see his beautiful face on the TV screen when I still could not take in the reality that I would never again see, touch, smell or hear my precious youngest child.

As he became older Daniel's love of music grew, he enjoyed a wide variety of music including indie, Britpop, trance, new wave and post punk. Daniel soon discovered music festivals including Creamfields and Nozstock which he attended regularly with an ever-growing circle of friends. The entrance tickets and bracelets still decorate his bedroom. I have no doubt that the music festivals he loved so much were where Dan first started to experiment with recreational drugs.

"Lord of the Rings" was his favourite movie - we had, as a family, seen the films in our local cinema as they were released and I will always remember Dan sitting entranced and motionless beside me for the whole three hours of the first film - he was just six years old. Daniel remained a fan of all the movies and watched all three films many times after that, eventually memorizing every word of the scripts by heart.

Through his teenage years Daniel became more rebellious, he cared little about what his teachers or anyone else thought of him, yet he always managed to achieve reasonable results for his school work and was never in any real trouble.

His teachers seemed to love him despite his carefree casual attitude. He was a natural mimic. After his death many of his friends told us stories (and recorded them in a memory book) of how he had entertained and amused them with his antics. Impossible for any of them to recall without falling into fits of giggles and unrestrained laughter.

I remember coming home one day when Dan was about thirteen years old to find that he had climbed on garden furniture, crawled over our glass conservatory roof and squeezed into his bedroom through a tiny open window. His reaction to my incredulous horror at the danger he had placed himself in was to shrug his shoulders and tell me that of course he was OK and that I shouldn't worry.

Daniel did poorly in his "A" levels after contracting glandular fever just before the exams. He "disappeared "into his room for six months, finally emerging to tell me he was re-sitting his exams and intended to apply for a course at Manchester Metropolitan University to study economics. I remember feeling so pleased and relieved, thinking that he was turning his life around and had a real sense of direction at last.

The call from the Manchester hospital came on the morning of February 19th 2016, Daniel was in his second term and had been at Manchester Met just five months. We drove as a family the 100 miles to Manchester in a state of extreme shock to find the strong, healthy twenty year old boy we had said goodbye to only the day before lying unconscious in ITU, attached to life support having suffered an out of hospital cardiac and respiratory arrest.

Gradually we put the pieces together to discover the full horror. Daniel had been using recreational drugs with increasing frequency during the five months he had been in Manchester. He had been out with his girlfriend partying the night before and she had woken to find him lifeless beside her. He had been resuscitated on the floor of his room in the university halls by paramedics and transferred to hospital.

For three days and nights we sat at his bedside hoping for a miracle that was not to be. Daniel was certified brain dead on February 21st at 3pm and the following morning became a multi-organ donor. I knew that Dan carried an organ donor card and I had talked about it with him when he put himself on the register three years earlier. I was the one who broached the subject with the ITU staff. It was not my decision but one that Daniel had made for himself. Even so it was very hard to sit at his bedside on that last night while the transplant coordinator informed me of each organ that she found a match for. In the end Daniel gave five organs to four different people, all of whom were at the top of the transplant list and had only days to live.

The following months remain a blur, a grey fog of grief that never lifted. I truly believed that I could not survive such horrendous pain, and find it hard to accept that I have now survived for three years. I remember walking around with my arms wrapped around my body, walking very slowly and carefully, feeling mortally wounded. The physical pain in my chest was so intense that I was sure my heart could not possibly keep beating and I welcomed the thought that death would relieve me from this pain. There was a constant screaming in my head "not my child, not my child". I thought I was losing my mind. Eventually I came to realize that this was not a real voice but just my own never-ending thoughts. The voice is quieter now, but it never really stops.

Somehow we survived the funeral, clearing out his university room, the inquest which confirmed that Daniel had died due to an accidental overdose of prescription drugs that he had obtained from the illegal market; all terrible days merged together in a dark sea of pain. A week after the funeral I fell headfirst down stairs suffering crush fractures to my right arm and damage to my inner ear. I barely remember it now despite surgery and many months of physio, lost in the fog. Many people were very kind; the constant supply of cooked meals from my sister and friends of Daniel will never be forgotten.

I remember lovingly reading and displaying so many cards and letters from so many people, the smell of the beautiful flowers that filled the house, my main purpose in life now to change the water and rearrange the blooms. I felt isolated, as if I was walking round in a bubble, invisible and forever on the outside looking in on a world I no longer understood or belonged in.

Eventually I discovered books on grief, on child loss, on sudden death and I started to read. From those books I found my way to the Compassionate Friends; it felt like a lifeline after four months to talk to mothers like me, who were surviving this nightmare.

I also journaled: one I wrote to Daniel, telling him all the things I would now never be able to, all the hopes and fears that I had kept hidden in my heart now poured out onto the empty pages. I also kept a second journal where I simply wrote down my feelings. Here I tried to record three things a day that I was thankful for. Simple things like the sound of birdsong, the aroma of fresh coffee or perhaps the sight of a butterfly passing by. My idea was to find something positive in a world that now seemed so dark and uncertain.

My husband left without warning over the first anniversary of Daniel's death. I was devastated, it felt like another bereavement, the only other person in the world who had lost what I had lost, who was with me when Daniel came into this world and with me when he left it, was gone. I turned, of course, to TCF Forum for support.

Eventually during that first year without my husband I came to realize that now at last I could confront the shame and guilt that I felt over the way Daniel had died. My now ex-husband had refused to talk about Dan's use of drugs, had encouraged me to tell people that his death was cardiac, and had refused to allow the funeral donations to go to help other young drug users as I had wanted.

To face up to a "stigmatized" death takes courage, courage that I finally found during my second year without Daniel. For so long I had felt angry and confused that the drug dealers on the streets of Manchester who sold my child a lethal dose of drugs were going unpunished and not pursued by the police. I now understand that until drug supply is taken out of the hands of criminals and properly regulated by government our children will continue to die. We will never stop young people experimenting with drugs, but it is our duty to reduce the risk of harm as much as possible.

Two years after Daniel's death I attended my first meeting with "Anyone's Child Families for Safer Drug Control", an activist group made up of people (mainly parents) whose lives have been wrecked by current UK drug laws and who campaign to change them. As the name suggests, the next death caused by drugs can be anyone's child - rich or poor, any colour or creed, there is no distinction. Our vision is that drugs will eventually be controlled by medical professionals, making drug use a medical issue instead of a criminal one as it is now.

When I wrote my story for their website I confronted all the painful truths surrounding Daniel's death that I had avoided and hidden from for so long. It was cathartic. I am now a member of Anyone's Child and with them I campaign for changes to our drug laws. I have met my MP, given media interviews and attended a rally in Westminster last June on World Drug Day. We believe that our power lies in the telling of our stories and that the changes in drug legislation we now see in many parts of the world will eventually reach our own country.

Daniel's friends organize a memorial football tournament every summer to remember him. We raise money and perhaps more importantly we raise awareness that harm from drugs is a problem for everyone. When Daniel died there were seven accidental deaths from drug overdose a day in the UK. Now, three years later, that figure has risen to ten per day. And so it will continue until our drug laws are based on harm reduction and protecting our children instead of punishment and criminalization.

Now when I see Daniel's face on the posters of Anyone's Child I feel proud that my son is helping to make the world a safer place for all of our children.

GUY JOSEPH
4.10.1986 to 14.10.2011

Our son Guy Joseph was killed in a paragliding accident in Spain on 14th October 2011 at the age of 25. He had lived his short life to the fullest, having experiences that most people only dream of and he died doing what he loved. Guy was born on 4th October 1986, a boy after two daughters, then aged four and half and six. Memories of his early years are a little hazy but I recall a very cute, independent and self-sufficient toddler. Guy had plenty of friends but was content to play alone, always more interested in making or building things than kicking a football around.

He was a bright, if somewhat lazy student but did well enough to gain a place at the local grammar school, then onto sixth-form college where he thrived. At the age of 16 he learned to Scuba dive and was instantly hooked. From then on, each summer he set off to advance his qualifications in some new exotic destination until he became an instructor.

When it was time to decide on a university course, the choice was obvious - a degree in Marine Biology would allow him access to the underwater world he loved and in 2006 he went up to study at Newcastle. His time at university was the usual beer-filled, friends-filled riot although, seemingly with little effort, he managed to achieve a first class degree.

A few weeks after graduating, Guy, determined to turn his passion into a job, and with the courage to leave his home comforts, set off for Indonesia to teach diving in the remote Togean Islands. I asked him how long he thought he'd be away – "a year, two years, five years, forever?" He shrugged and said: "somewhere between the last two". I never dreamed that 'forever' would be literal.

Without Internet or phone, and with few English speakers around, he taught himself Indonesian and adopted three local orphaned puppies who followed him around adoringly; as it seems did a fair number of the female dive students who passed through!

After six months in the Togeans, Guy worked in East Timor and then found another diving instructor job on the Indonesian Island of Flores. After almost two years there he felt he needed a change and having read a magazine article about paragliding in Nepal, headed up to the Himalayas during the winter break from diving. In Nepal he met a fellow Englishman who owned a paragliding school in Spain and was in the process of opening another in Dubai. He offered Guy the job of managing the Dubai school and invited him to Spain to learn the ropes of the business. He went back to Indonesia, handed in his notice and in September 2011 came home for two weeks before heading off to Spain.

Tragically, just three weeks later, on a bright Friday afternoon, six paragliders set out but only five returned. Guy's body was found the following morning in a wooded valley just a kilometer away from the agreed landing place. The cause of death was hypovolemic shock, although we will never know exactly what happened.

I will never forget the moment I heard the news. Our younger daughter had been staying with us, convalescing after a mastectomy and we were already in a slightly fragile state after her breast cancer diagnosis. She and I had been in central London for the afternoon and then went our separate ways, her to meet some friends and me to cycle home. As I rode towards our house, a taxi pulled up and our elder daughter emerged. I was confused; I'd seen her the previous day, why was she here? Then I saw my younger daughter in the kitchen with two police officers; what was going on?

Guy had lived away from home for a number of years and so we felt we didn't truly know him as an adult. However, as tributes poured in from around the world, we learned just how much he was loved and were overwhelmed by how much his adventurous lifestyle and his wise, gentle character inspired people. We saw that beyond the excitement and the fun-filled life was a kind, patient, compassionate young man who was an unfalteringly loyal friend.

The moment that I heard the news of Guy's death will be etched on my memory forever but shock has a way of numbing your emotions (perhaps it's the only way you can survive) and all I remember of my thoughts at that time is that I knew, literally within minutes, that we had to do something to keep Guy's name alive. I had absolutely no idea what that something would be or how we would do it, but I knew that I had to salvage something from this catastrophe. Now that he could no longer achieve anything in his life, I felt I had to do it for him, to find meaning in his death and in some way realise his lost potential.

Where to start? We organised a brainstorming meeting. Fifteen of Guy's friends from different parts of his life – university, school, childhood friends, people he'd met on his travels, many of them previously unknown to us – came together to help decide on a fitting legacy for their friend. As one by one they introduced themselves, saying how they knew Guy, the irony of the fact that they were only with us because he wasn't, seemed almost unbearable.

After much discussion, two ideas began to emerge - we would fund a project to support marine conservation in Indonesia and we would build a facility of some kind for children in Nepal. Now 'all' we had to do was to find two suitable projects, think of a name for our new charity, register it with the Charities Commission and HMRC, design a logo, create a website, set up social media accounts and an online donation facility, have T-shirts and collection cans made... and raise some money! Five months after Guy's death Guy's Trust was born.

Finding a suitable marine conservation project was the easy part. Guy was one of the founder members of MantaWatch, an organisation dedicated to monitoring and protecting the endangered manta ray. In consultation with his colleagues we agreed to fund two internships for young Indonesian marine science students to spend a month in Flores, where Guy lived, working for MantaWatch, conducting research on mantas and at the same time furthering their studies and careers.

The internship programme has gone from strength to strength and we have now funded over 30 students. The MantaWatch alumni are really making Guy's dreams a reality. Seeing photographs of young Indonesian students in Guy's Trust T-shirts on the boat on which Guy worked and where we had spent two holidays with him is both poignant and hugely rewarding; we know he would be so chuffed!

Finding a project in Nepal was clearly going to be more challenging. We were fully aware of the necessity of meeting an existing need and of the pitfalls of working in a developing country with no knowledge of the language or culture. We needed an established and experienced partner organisation, who would also understand our desire for a project to which we could attach Guy's name and the emotional journey that this would entail.

We finally chose ActionAid, an NGO with an excellent reputation for international development, whose proposal ticked every one of our boxes. We would build an Early Childhood Development Centre (ECDC), a pre-school facility for 25 children in the district where Guy lived, and not only fund it but take a group to actually start the construction ourselves. Despite our grief, we began to feel that life still had some point.

In November 2012 my husband Tony and I visited Nepal and met the Dalit (untouchable) community whose children would, for the first time, be able to attend school. They told us of their struggles, their gratitude for the life-changing opportunity Guy's Trust was giving their children, how sad they were for our loss and that "all of our children are your children too". And then we cried together, first for Guy and then for the better future their children would now have. It was a humbling experience.

And then in March 2013 we, our two daughters, and 27 friends from around the world converged on the small village in the foothills of the

Annapurna mountain range to spend a week digging the foundations for the first 'Guy Joseph ECDC'.

It is difficult to adequately describe the emotions of that week - from surveying a planeload of people in Guy's Trust T-shirts landing at Pokhara airport to standing on a Himalayan mountainside while a group of Nepali villagers asked us to join them for a minute's silence in memory of our son; from digging a trench with a team of Guy's friends to watching the paragliders over the distant lake where Guy had flown just two years earlier. So many moments of camaraderie, pride and yes, fun - but all underscored by a profound sadness.

What started as the germ of an idea rooted in the need to do something to keep Guy's name alive, has eight years on, resulted in raising over £900,000; building three Guy Joseph Early Childhood Development Centres and three libraries in Nepal, building five primary schools and a library in Cambodia, another country where Guy spent time, and the establishment of the Guy Joseph MantaWatch Awards in Indonesia.

On that dreadful day in October 2011, we decided simply that we had to create a tangible memorial to our beloved son and brother. Eight years on, Guy's Trust has grown beyond our wildest dreams, has become virtually a full time job for me, maintains contact with Guy's friends and also serves as a therapeutic diversion from our sadness. Guy's Trust seems to have an unstoppable momentum and is a fitting testament to a young man who had such an enormous zest for life and was loved by and inspired so many people. It has been a way of confronting our grief obliquely and a way to salvage meaning from the terrible waste of a life cut short.

CHARLIE CRAIG
10.11.2001 to 21.1.2017

My name is Sarah and my husband's Nick. My 2 boys Thomas and Charlie.

Charlie was born at 06.30am on the 10 November 2001, weighing 10llb.

He was a contented baby. He ate, slept and cried for food and nappy change. His brother Thomas, who was then 4 years old started school shortly after his birth. Our lives quickly changed from one child family to our completed family of 4.

I was a community nurse and Nick a professional mountain biker. I was lucky to be able to take a year out of work on maternity leave, however I only ever worked part time so that I could be at home with the boys. We had grandparent help whilst I worked.

Our lives had always been busy due to Nick's job of travel and competing. The boys soon got use to our life styles and thrived in them. Their ability to talk and socialize with adults and make new friends is something that I hope will always be a positive attribute for Thomas, as he grows into a young man. Charlie enjoyed his wide circle of friends as he grew within the cycling community of mountain bike and Cyclo-cross.

My husband had led a professional career in cycling and both boys soon showed natural talent in the sport.

Charlie unfortunately broke his femur when he was 8 years old, attempting a bike jump. We were airlifted to hospital where this determined little boy showed his true bravery towards the obstacles that were then put in front of him. Charlie's recovery was hard and slowly but surely after 4 months he was back on his bike and his crutches were cast aside.

Charlie always enjoyed school and had a large group of friends that sometimes led him to mischievousness. Charlies best friend Joe was 10 weeks older and in a different school year, but their friendship was strong and after school and weekends they would plan "stough" to do, usually involving mud, bikes, play bike, in-the-mud, Lego, Monopoly, games, cricket, river walking, snow, scouts, racing ,filming, cricket, running, swimming and just play. They entertained themselves with their own creations, Charlie often the creator.

Our family time was camping, with VW camper holidays, Wales, fishing, sea, crabs, mackerel, riding bikes, beach fires, stargazing and simple time spent outdoors costing nothing.

Yes, there were arguments, disagreements, a lot of testosterone as boys became teenagers.

Family Life was not all smiles but we tried to give the boys a sense of peace, love and adventure. They understood travel and the wider world, but they also appreciated the small things; the sunset, nature and family time.

Charlie enjoyed photography and film and loved to capture the moment. His photos would be compared and discussed with his dad and brother Thomas. This was something they all enjoyed sharing especially on their touring trips to France.

Charlie taught his dad and Thomas to fish for mackerel off the rocks, by thinking like a fish. He would watch them wriggle in a pool before he killed them for tea.

The day Charlie died.

I found Charlie about 11.00 am on a Saturday morning. Thinking he was having a lie in which was unusual. I checked on Charlie at 09.30 and he looked fast asleep with his face turning away from me, so I left him a bit longer. By 10.30 I went upstairs and started to make a bit of noise to wake him, but no response. I went in and said his name quietly, touched his arm and instantly felt that cold feeling. I looked at his skin, turned to his face and knew, I just knew. I screamed that mother's agonizing noise, the one you think animals do, the one you know when your child is dead.

This day has such painful emotions. Did it really happen? Has it happened? Has this happened to us? Our family. There are so many boys, why one of my precious boys, no, it's not true.

Denial, anger, refusal to accept, do I have to accept? But I know it's true, yet Charlie is real, he is real to me.

Our lives turned upside down.

Our lovely chatty, vibrant boy full of love, fun and determination to make the most of every day no matter what obstacles were in front of him.

Instantly we were asked about gifts of money, charities to send it to, who and what to support.

We wanted to support everything Charlie was, is. We wanted to give what Charlie aspired to. We wanted others to get a glimpse of his full exciting mind that drove us all to utter exhaustion. We wanted those young people in the future to hear Charlie's name and ask who he was.

We wanted Charlie to make a difference. So with the help of our dear friends we set up a fund to help support young people to experience off road cycling events and non-racing events as Charlie did. "RideforCharlie" evolved and with it WWW.rideforcharlie.com. We also wanted to support the amazing C-R-Y charity in memory of Charlie to allocate heart screening days for young people aged 14-35.

Our friends, people that have heard of us and Charlie started raising money.

Money started rolling in, people challenging themselves and awareness of Charlie spreading national and world wide.

We have raised around £20,000 for C-R-Y, put aside for heart screening, and around £100.000 for "RideforCharlie". This has been amazing and very emotional as emails come in weekly expressing their heartfelt emotions for us.

The awareness of heart screening from the age of 14-35, was something we had not heard of. C-R-Y is a charity that does screening for young people and awareness of heart conditions that people wouldn't be aware of.

As Charlie died suddenly, he had a post mortem and his heart was sent to St George's Hospital for Dr. Sheppard to examine. They then invited the 3 of us to go for screening ourselves to see if they could find a link with our hearts and Charlie's. However, this did not result in any possible diagnosis for Charlie and the research team continued to try and answer our questions.

A coroner's inquest attempted to conclude why our lovely boy died.

Following the inquest, recommendations were given to British Cycling, as a positive way forward for change in the future.

They have since put in place heart screening recommendations for any 14 year old and above on the British cycling pathway. We have also suggested information on Heart screening and C-R-Y in the membership packs issued to all members of British cycling. This is on-going as they are working closely with C-R-Y to decide the best way of incorporating this information.

We are keeping in touch with the membership department and are hoping that Charlie's picture stands as a lasting memory within British cycling, so that he is remembered always.

We have Charlie to thank for he has left us with so much to learn from.

People often say how do you carry on? I don't know. We get up, put the coffee machine on and start our day. Some days are incredibly hard, emotionally and physically. It's tiring and pulls at you in so many ways. I have my incredible husband to thank for his positivity and Charlie's drive for life each day. We thank Charlie for his love .Yet there are days, many of them, when it's hard to get out of bed clean your teeth and put the coffee on. Thomas our other brave loving son is our other reason to carry on. We think of him and how hard he is working for his degree and he gives us the determination to live for the future. We have to hope the future is brighter and Charlie is with us always. We are a family of four and always will be.

DEBBIE ROOKE
22.1.1982 to 13.4.2013

Debbie was born on 22nd January 1982 in Rochford Hospital, a first child for David and I. Both sets of proud grandparents were long-term Avenue Baptist Church members. Debbie had the privilege of being dedicated at the first service that the Rev. Alan Griggs conducted at Avenue. Avenue was a big part of Debbie's young life. She was taken out to crèche on a Sunday morning from a few weeks old, and attended the young wives group crèche mid-week. As she grew she went into beginners.

Debbie attended Westborough Primary School, then Prittlewell High, then went on to Westcliff High to study A-levels.

All this time Debbie had been involved in all the activities at Avenue, and was taught in Sunday school by a number of our current members. Debbie was an independent thinker and she did not see being brought up in the church as a good enough reason to become a Christian or be baptised. She spent much time investigating Christianity and seeking answers before deciding to accept Christ in her late teens and later being baptised at Avenue.

After obtaining excellent grades in A-Levels, she went to Keele University to study Biology and Biochemistry. At University she quickly made friends. One of her first friends was Julie, who was also a Christian, and together they joined the Christian Union. Julie would remain one of her closest friends for the rest of her life.

After two years at Keele, as part of her Degree, Debbie went to work at the Natural History Museum in Paris, despite only having French to GCSE level. Within six months, Debbie was fluent in French and helping others having trouble making themselves understood.

She returned to do her final year at Keele, achieving a First Class Honours degree, before spending some time on Iona. Debbie had been unsure where God wanted her, and had been considering medicine, or some sort of scientific research. However she came back from Iona with a clear idea that it was teaching that she was being led towards. She went back to Keele to do a PGCE, and during this time also decided to become a Catholic. She returned to Southend to find work and began working at King John School in Benfleet. It was then that she began attending St Helen's Church regularly.

Before Debbie left Avenue, she felt that she wanted to give something back for all that Avenue had given her as she grew up. For a number of years, Debbie had had an obsession with all things Titanic. This was even before the blockbuster film came out. She had collected all sorts of memorabilia and started to live and breathe Titanic. Debbie came to a realisation that her obsession was affecting her relationship with God and with her friends. She made a decision to get rid of all the memorabilia. She sold it all and used the profits to help buy some new furniture for the youth lounge at the church - sofas, rugs and beanbags, which were all greatly appreciated by the Bible Class and youth group at the time. Even after leaving Avenue, Deb would still sometimes be seen in our pews on special occasions such as Christmas or Mother's Day.

She would also sometimes come into coffee with us after the St Helen's service had finished.

Debbie was always busy and became more involved with St Helen's, particularly with the Legion of Mary, visiting various members of the parish. She also did a first aid course and trained to become a St John's Ambulance volunteer.

After some time working at Cecil Jones School, she moved to De La Salle in Basildon and immediately felt at home there. She decided that she wanted to train in helping children with dyslexia and took a 2-year course. As part of this she did some tutoring and from a card we have had since her death it appears to have been very successful.

Debbie did not see the long summer holiday as the chance to go and lie on a beach for a few weeks. Instead each year she would look for some challenge to fill the summer. One year she went to Uganda to help build a school, another she spent renovating a house. Yet another was spent on an 800-mile bike ride to raise money for a brain tumour charity that had been set up in memory of her old school friend Sarah. In the summer of 2013 she had planned another charity bike-ride with Kris, a friend she had met during a pilgrimage in the New Year break.

Deb's last adventure was a cycling and camping trip to Norfolk, taking in a visit to the shrine at Walsingham. It was during the Easter holidays, early April, but absolutely freezing. She was determined to go - it was a practice run really for her planned summer cycle-ride. She texted a friend from the campsite: 'Strange really - loads of caravans, but mine's the only tent - can't think why'.

Sadly, Debbie never made it back from that camping trip. She visited the shrine at Walsingham, and was heading back to her campsite at Swaffham when she was hit by a car coming in the opposite direction.

No more can be said about the circumstances of the accident, but the police family liaison officer reassured David and I that she had been doing nothing wrong. Despite quick thinking on the part of the first person on the scene, the efforts of all the emergency services, including the East Anglian Air Ambulance, and the Neuro Critical Care Unit at Addenbrooke's Hospital, Cambridge, Debbie's injuries were too severe.

My husband David, Simon, her brother, the wider family and all those who knew her, were devastated. Those days after 13th April 2013 felt very dark and tested many people's faith. However, even then there was a spark of hope. She was on the organ donor register and it was hoped that despite her injuries some of her organs may be able to be used for transplant, or at least for medical research relating to other transplants. We have since heard that Debbie's lungs have been given to a woman in her twenties with cystic fibrosis who had not been expected to survive much longer. Her corneas gave two people the gift of sight also.

Coverage of Debbie's accident and her life on BBC Radio Essex and in the Southend Evening Echo was an incredible witness to the wider community - much of the following paragraph from her eulogy was printed in the Echo article on the funeral.

Deb made time for everyone. Her faith was at the centre of all she did. She had so much energy and drive, using every minute of every day. She didn't seem to know the meaning of standing still. So many things will be missed about Deb, but her smile, her enthusiasm, boundless energy and her willingness to help absolutely anyone are high on the list. She made a difference in the world in a way that few of us can ever hope to do. She valued education and never stopped learning, but the way she lived was not because of **what** she knew, but **who** she knew - that is our Lord and Saviour, Jesus Christ. The best way we can honour Deb's memory is to get to know Jesus for ourselves and try to be Christ-like in how we treat those around us.

About 400 people attended her funeral, from all over the country and members from St Helen's and Avenue came together in a memorable way. Contributions were made to the East Anglian Air Ambulance and the Neuro Critical Care Unit at Addenbrooke's in Debbie's memory. Debbie, we found, had had a monthly standing order to Mary's Meals, a Charity that helps underprivileged children abroad to attend school, therefore get an education, health checks and school meals, which means that in the future they will get jobs and the cycle will be changed for that family!!!

Debbie's aunt wrote a book on her life and all the profits plus costs went to the Debbie Rooke Memorial Fund which mainly went to Mary's Meals, in total more than £10,000 with a friend of Debbie', Kris, doing a Sponsored cycle ride in her memory too. This fund also supported for 5 years, prizes at the school she worked at, prizes for children who had achieved despite the odds against them in various ways. Dave and I presented these at the school each year for 5 years. A childhood friend called Judd ran in the London Marathon and raised about £1000 for St

Johns ambulance (Debbie was a volunteer) and Judd has since trained and become one too.

A bench in her memory is in place at Walsingham Shrine, Norfolk and another bench is placed in St Helen's Church chapel garden, where Debbie was an active member. Also her books and photo are in the chapel in her memory. The biggest legacy to Debbie in some ways though, is in me setting up a group for bereaved parents in 2015, 2 years after Debbie died. This group very soon became part of The Compassionate Friends and still is and has helped many parents over those years, many of whom still attend and are in contact.

CAMILLA CADLE
28.4.1991 to 6.8.1998

Camilla was born on the 28th April 1991 and at the age of 20 months, after the deaths of her parents, she joined our family on 12th December 1992. Her father, my brother, had died 6 weeks previously and her mother 3 weeks after her father's death.

My brother wrote a diary during the 9 months on the run up to his death. It described what was a very volatile relationship he had with Camilla's mother. I only have his side of the story. My GP referred to it as the type of relationship that you can't live with the person but neither can you live without them. The result of which was both of their deaths.

Camilla had seen and heard things that a baby and young toddler should never have to witness. From my brother's diary it would seem there were many arguments, there was destruction of belongings and there was physical assault and mental abuse within his relationship with Camilla's mother. All practically on a daily basis with the odd bit of respite in between. Camilla had been traumatised all of her short 20 months of life and now she had lived with family members who were not well known to her after the death of her mother and three weeks later and over a 500 mile drive she was in our care. We were related but total strangers to her which added to her state of trauma. I would go so far as to say that she probably suffered from post-traumatic stress disorder but this was not recognised in children in those days.

Children might forget about troubling and traumatic events but their organs, muscles and spirits do not. Research now indicates that Adverse Childhood Events (ACEs) can alter the way the child reacts to daily stressors. With multiple ACEs, the child's brain development may be stunted leading to a lack of self-awareness and cognitive deficiencies. The scars are not visible but can and do put ACE children at a high risk for serious mental, physical, emotional and social health complications. After a year in our care we had noticed that Camilla had little self-awareness, lack of fear, could be moody in extreme, had difficulty keeping friends and non-stop talking to name a few of the ramifications that her early childhood had on her.

Camilla was a very vulnerable toddler who was filled with fear and reacted accordingly. She had a sickly pale complexion, had little hair on her head but what was there was very blonde but looked non-existent which didn't help her good looks. She had the most stunning coloured eyes which were a soft green with flecks of other colours through them. I have never seen this eye colour before or since. She was certainly unique.

The first few months living with us she did nothing but sing songs to her favourite TV programmes which were Thomas the Tank Engine, Neighbours [!] and Sooty. She also soothed herself by cuddling into a large soft toy, would pick fluff off her jumpers with her thumb and forefinger and did this to another soft toy which was, by the time she grew out of doing this, 98% bare.

We discovered our parenting skills were of no use to Camilla and by the time she was 3 realised we were needing help to manage her. Repeating yourself, made no difference to the outcome. Giving her consequences didn't work either. Telling her that she was too young to walk to school at age 5 and she disagreeing with you every day of her short time at school. This was due to all her trauma and losses as it was not just her parents, it was her home, her surroundings, her belongings as her mother had disposed of most of them, then the move before she came to us.

It added up to a young girl whose brain had not been nurtured leading it to form differently from those that have received nurturing. At that time, we were just beginning to recognise and acknowledge that this could come under the heading of Camilla not being able to attach to us and would be described now as having Attachment Problems with Post Traumatic Stress Disorder.

Fast forward to 1996. She was in her first year of primary school and enjoying it. Considering what she had been through she was bright, very clever, had no problems with education and picked it up easily. This was all interrupted after a few months in her first term when she was sent home from school as she was ill. Both my husband and I had taken her to our doctor many times over the previous few months as she was not recovering well from a cold and on top of that a vaccination booster for school.

We could also see that some days she looked very unwell and though she complained of a sore stomach, was able to eat her food. She also developed a limp! This limp seemed to come and go though. One final attendance at our doctors and before we knew it we were heading to the local Children's Hospital.

We were kept in hospital while x-rays, scans, blood tests, ultra sounds, etc., were done before we were officially told that Camilla was indeed very ill. She had Neuroblastoma, which is a rare type of cancer that mostly affects babies and young children usually under the age of 5. Camilla had turned 5 a few months before this. Good Luck was not on her side at all. Before we knew it we were heading to the cancer ward and dreading what lay ahead for her and ourselves. It would be a further 6 weeks before we were able to return home with Camilla. Our thoughts were "Surely she has been through enough and that she must survive this as life was being very cruel to her indeed". Camilla was already at Stage 4 and given a couple of months to live. However, if she was given chemotherapy, an operation to remove the tumour, radiotherapy, radiation treatment, a bone marrow transplant then she may have a 10% chance of survival!

Hospital was extremely difficult for her. There were too many new faces, there were too many blood tests taken, there were too many plasters that had to be changed and the treatment was grueling for her. She made her mark though with many of the doctors and nurses and she certainly made them work hard for their money.

She was not the easiest of patients and the poor teacher used to be frightened to see her and would avoid her at all costs! Camilla had a method of easily upsetting people that she just met. Her comments could stun you and you would wonder what on earth you had done or said for her to react in this way to you. It was Camilla's way of survival. If you stayed long enough she would then warm to you and could be a joy to be with after this initial meeting. Some people never got past this test! This could happen every time you met her.

One of the comical situations we had was a few days after Camilla was admitted she was to have an ultrasound done on her tummy. The ultrasound doctor was not very child friendly and just got on with his job sticking the gel on her tummy and then the instrument without very much preparation. He didn't have the time to waste with bedtime manners on her or to get to know her enabling Camilla to relax a little.

She had been squeezed in on his very busy schedule and he wanted his lunch that morning not mid -afternoon! However, Camilla decided to start screaming her head off while she was trying to get away from what she thought were his clawing hands and started pushing herself up the top of the bed and at the same time screaming "HE'S KILLING ME, HELP HE'S KILLING ME!" over, and over again. I have to say in her defence that the area he was scanning was very sore to be touched as the tumour which had grown on her adrenal gland was now the size of a large grapefruit and swelling into her other organs pushing them out of place.

We tried to console and distract her, but she was in fight, flight or in her case, scream mode and would not quieten down. Camilla's brain was in a zone that could not be reached and nothing was going to stop her screaming.

The doctor finished as quickly as he could to get her away from his room. It wasn't until the double doors of his room were opened and Camilla, in her bed, was pushed through them that we saw the queue outside! The children were waiting with their parents to have their ultrasounds done.

Everyone's eyes were staring on the child that came out from that room and through the door. Everybody was silent. Everybody was tense. You could see the fear on the children's faces and in their eyes as they wondered what on earth was going to happen to them. Everybody was dreading seeing this doctor that had tried to kill the child that had just come out of the room! These poor parents would indeed have problems getting their children to go in to see this doctor as after all he had tried to kill the last child in there! We didn't envy the parents and staff the task ahead of them to get the next victim, sorry patient, into that room without some sort of protest. We walked smugly away thanking God we were now through that bit of examination but snorting on the inside at the turmoil Camilla had created. She could be quite a Drama Queen.

There were many low points during the next 12 months or so but so long as she was receiving treatment she was alive. It gave us time to cherish what days/nights we had with her. We continued to think that she had to survive this as life could not be this cruel to her. Well, life was that cruel. In May 1998 we were advised after a short stay in the hospital that there was no more that could be done for her and that she would not survive.

Our worst nightmare was happening. We were shocked, stunned, numb, lost for words. After the news was delivered to us we had been told that we could go home immediately! We had to leave the doctor's office and return to Camilla after receiving this news not having time for it to sink in, not having time to put a "brave face" on. The tears were pouring out of my eyes, there was fear and dread on hubby's face as we walked towards Camilla.

We had to return to the ward that we shared with 5 other families. We avoided other parent's eyes and members of staff as we did not want to have to share the awful news that we had been given. We still could not believe it. We had to face Camilla and pretend all was well, collect her belongings packing them into bags wiping the tears away so that she didn't see them. Camilla was delighted we were heading home as this was the best place for her to be.

Hubby and I could not talk, were frightened to look at each other as it was too easy to break down.

The journey home was horrendous as what we had been told was still sinking in plus we had the task of telling our two children, then the rest of the family and friends of the up to date situation and what would we tell Camilla. How do you break this news to a six year old child?

Within a couple of months Camilla's body faded away and eventually let her down. Her spirit never wavered. She would give our doctor a run for his money, she hated the nurses touching her and fiddling with her equipment. She was demanding, awkward and antagonistic to all but she had reason to be like this. She just wanted to be left alone.

She got that right on the morning of the 6th August 1998 when she died.

During the following weeks, months, years help and support was sought at different times for all of us. I eventually persuaded or should I say, blackmailed my son and daughter to attend a weekly event that was being run by Tak Tent (a Scottish charity that had been set up to help cancer patients and their families). They had a special group for teenagers and young adults and Tak Tent were running a course on self-esteem. I promised them that they could both stop once the course was finished but until then they were to attend. They reluctantly agreed and by the end of the 8 weeks they had made some firm friends within the group. Over the next ten years or so our children made the most of Tak Tent and there were times when funds needed to be raised for trips, annual conferences, etc. This was when hubby and I would help out.

After Camilla's death discussions were held about what we could do in memory of her but nothing got off the ground and so long as we were helping Tak Tent we felt that this was enough. We really didn't have the energy, the get up and go that you need to push yourself to do something extra. We were still adjusting to life without Camilla.

However, having spent several years in managing Camilla's difficult moods, disruptive behaviour, non-stop talking, food fads, phobias and a whole lot more we wondered if fostered children could benefit from the skills and experiences we had picked up along the way. We didn't dive into it straight away but about 5 years later started the long process of becoming foster carers. After 18 months we were approved and eventually completed 11 years of foster caring with a national charity.

During these 11 years our first fostered child came to live with us on the 13th December 2004 (Camilla arrived on 12th December

1992). This to me was a good Omen. He was aged 9, a lovely child to look after, though he had his difficulties. He would always listen to advice and then do his best. His mum died of cancer when he was just 21 so he stayed with us for an extra year or so to help him during this difficult time. He now lives in his own flat and has a full time job. We meet up with him to see how he is doing and make sure he is not struggling on his own.

Our second child came for a 2 night respite and forgot to go back! He did return for a few weeks but the family he was with were having great difficulties with him. We did not find these problems and accepted him until he was adopted two years later at age 4. He was very loving, talked to anybody, and had the most stunning blue eyes and blonde hair. Our problem was keeping up with him! He ran everywhere and was on the go as most toddlers are but we were of an age that we found it quite hard to keep up with him! His adoption went ahead and we are so lucky in that his parents have maintained contact with us. He is now the same height as me, still has his beautiful blue eyes and growing into a lovely young man.

Our third child was the younger brother of our first. Boy did he find it difficult to fit in. This child was allowed to do what he wanted at home so our rules, not that we had many, were challenged daily. This would be about his bedtime, washing himself, brushing his teeth, etc. He took many months to settle but he got there. He returned to his mum after 18 months with us. After this we had another boy (who arrived on Camilla's Birthday!) for 2 years who was the size of a 10 year old but was only 8. He returned to a family member.

Then a girl who was aged 10 but looked about 6. When I was helping this child to unpack I discovered an ornament that her mother had given her was the exact same as the ornament we had put on Camilla's grave for her 21st Birthday! This child had many problems settling and though we were highlighting them they were being ignored. Unfortunately for all of us this child had to be placed in a residential home. It took us about 18 months before we could meet up with her again and continue to do so a few times each year. This is letting her know that we still want to be part of her life even though she can't live with us. She has recently left school and secured a job which I hope will be the start of a better life for her.

Looking after traumatised children is extremely wearing on your nerves and mental health. You do not always have the understanding of other professionals and parents who judge you and the child. The gap to recover from our last child became longer and longer and it came to a point where we enjoyed our home being peaceful, no arguments being created by other people and wondering what "mood" would be flying in through the back door after school came out. Reluctantly we decided to retire from fostering but, on the whole, thoroughly enjoyed living with our fostered children who we learnt so much from. Each, and every one of them a blessing. If Camilla had not stepped into our lives then we would never have fostered other children so we see Fostering as part of her legacy too.

Like most parents' roles it is a thankless task and you have to pray and hope that the impact and influence you had on each child will help them in their future. They have experienced a "normal" (well this might be disputed!) home life and it is this that we hope they take from us giving them the tools for any family they may go on to have in the future. We both got tremendous satisfaction from helping the children who have lived with us leaving many, some sad, but mostly funny and very rewarding memories of each and every child.

Fast forward to 6th August 2018 where we would be commemorating 20 years without Camilla I took the decision to do something "special" but what I was not sure at all.

I had mentioned it to my hubby who came up with no clear ideas and possibly wanted it to just pass by quietly. He then heard about Random Acts of Kindness and how "I should do some"! I was a bit peeved about this as he is always the last person to put his hand in his pocket to give any of his cash away in that he doesn't tip waiting staff or hairdressers, etc., unless I remind him to.

Shortly after this we were stuck indoors for many days as we had had a heavy fall of snow and the village was cut off. On the fourth day of snow I suggested we walk to the village cafe for lunch. Off we went in our heavy boots and muffled up as it was bitterly cold. At the cafe we ordered lunch and while waiting for it to arrive two of our local "Rescue Team" came in and sat down near us to have a break and a bite to eat to keep them going. I asked them if they had been busy to which they said that they were utterly exhausted as they hadn't stopped since the snow started (we were into the fourth day/night by then). They also mentioned how thoughtless and irresponsible some members of the public were as they took stupid risks to drive when advised to stay home.

We ate our meal, said goodbye to the men and went to pay our dues. Outside the cafe I reminded hubby about the Random Acts of Kindness and was surprised that he hadn't thought to pay for the men's snacks from the Rescue Team. "That's a brilliant idea" said husband. "I wished I'd have thought of that. Do you think I should?" I said it was up to him so he returned and paid for the men's snacks. Boy did he feel good about this Random Act of Kindness especially the next day when we bumped into a member of the public who was in the cafe at the same time as us and who had heard the waitress tell both Rescue Men that their snacks had been paid for.

The men were delighted, gave them a boost and how happy it had made them. I thought, "Trust him to get feed-back on his first Random Act of Kindness!" The snow disappeared and life returned to normal but I still yearned to do something positive for somebody else in memory of Camilla but didn't know what.

Each month of that year I would look out for a charity or local fundraiser and give sums of money to them without letting on to HUBBY!!! The money was going all over the place, some within the village for a young girl who needed to raise funds to buy a therapy dog as she was Autistic. More was sent to "Facing Africa' where surgeons travel to Africa to perform complex facial reconstruction surgery on children. Purchasing a few bricks for Father's Day to help build toilets in Africa, and so on. However nothing was giving me a purpose to do or give more that was until I came across a film titled "Tashi and the Monk". Out of curiosity I watched it as I wondered why a Buddhist monk would be involved with a young girl.

The film introduced you to Lobsang Phunstok who had received the honour of being trained under the guidance of His Holiness the Dalai Lama. Lobsang Phunstok's objective was to share Tibetan Buddhism with the West and had been living in America to do so. He did not find contentment with this and left behind a life as a spiritual teacher in the USA to create a unique community in the foothills of the Himalayas which rescues orphaned and neglected children.

What an impact this had on me. Tashi was new to the community and just didn't fit in. She was unsettled, she was unhappy, she fought with other children, was struggling to understand why she was there. Tashi reminded me of my daughter, Camilla and the struggles she had in life which were parallel to Tashi's.

Over many months Tashi's life was filmed and at the end you saw her adjusting to life within the community. You saw that she was making friends something that she could not do on her arrival. You could see that she had a bright future ahead of her now and that Lobsang Phunstok and the staff that help run the community had, with love and compassion, been able to save this child from a life of hardship, of being misunderstood, giving her a happy and fulfilling life and one with a positive future

After watching the film I just had to find out more about this community that sits on a remote mountain top called "Jhamtse Gatsal" (Tibetan for The Garden of Love and Compassion). The more I discovered the more I was impressed with Lobsang Phunstok's vision for the community he was creating, but most importantly was the number of children he was educating, feeding, clothing and giving shelter to which, at the present time, is 80. I had huge admiration for this man, his vision and how he was accomplishing it with the help of supporters from around the world.

This took me to the website of Jhamtse Gatsal (www.jhamtsegatsal.org) and found that you could sponsor a child and thought this is what I wanted to do. I contacted the American arm of this community to find out more. I thought I would be allocated a child but I was sent a list of children with their photographs who needed sponsoring. Selecting "one" of them was the most difficult thing to do. It took me several visits to this page as it was so hard to choose just one.

As time grew closer to the 6th August 2018 I settled on one young girl and applied. My husband and I are now one of her sponsors. She will be heading to university in a few years' time. We will help her get through this stage in her life and once she is able to stand on her own two feet we will help another child. I hope that she will love to travel and come and meet us one day in the future.

Now that we have established a link with her we do have sporadic contact with her. Where they live they rely on Westerners visiting to take the post to them as there is no local postal service to do this. It makes it a very special day, almost like a holiday for the children in the community, when they receive small gifts, letters and most importantly, photos of their sponsors. It makes such a difference to them that there are adults in this world that want to help them. We also have to wait until a Westerner returns and then we get letters, cards, and photos of what our child has done since the last contact. These contacts bring you to tears of joy as you know that your small contribution is making a huge difference to one young person's future and life.

On the morning of 6th August 2018 the day Camilla had died 20 years earlier, I handed my husband a card with all the little and big Random Acts of Kindness that he had generously contributed to over the previous 8 months but knew nothing about! His face was a picture when he saw the total at the bottom of it. He gulped once or twice before he could speak. I then said you need to read about our sponsored child, watch the film and it will make sense to you why I have chosen this community.

Just before Christmas we received many photos of our child one of which I have in a frame in our lounge and hubby shows it off telling everybody about her as if he had done it all himself!!! He won't admit it to me but he is secretly quite proud of the impact that he is having on another child's future.

This legacy has brought us great happiness, in touch with a young person who lives many thousands of miles away from us in a very remote part of the world. Her contact with us is greatly treasured and we hope that the effect on this young girl will have a rippling effect in her life, the community that she will belong to and most importantly any children that she may one day have.

From utter despair with the loss of our daughter, Camilla, grows something strong, positive and having an impact that is life-long for generations to come.

GEORGE TSAFTAROPOULOS
8.6.1984 to 20.3.2012

I was an only child born to elderly Greek parents whom I lost very early on in my life. The Greek relatives, wanting to see me safely settled into marriage, quickly organised proxies for me, which was the custom of the times. My husband was introduced to me and we were betrothed, marrying a stranger two months later.

It was a very unhappy marriage but gave me three beautiful boys whom I cherished and lived my life through. George was my second son and was born on the 8th June 1984.

He was a strikingly beautiful baby in colouring, with strawberry blonde hair, pink skin and auburn eyes. He was a standout in the family of dark haired olive skinned Greeks. He was always a very quiet child, but loving.

We moved to Greece to appease my Greek born hubby and struggled three years in an unfriendly and unfamiliar environment with particularly difficult struggles with his family. Being the subject of abuse both physically and emotionally, eventually I escaped back to Australia with three kids under ten in tow.

The first few months we were sleeping on floors and eating church handouts. My husband came back and then left again several times over the years. I worked, established a home and put my three boys through school. It was in high school that my George, at the age of 17, a straight "A" student, school prefect, first developed depression through stress at school, being stalked and bullied, and his girlfriend committing suicide so he developed mental health issues.

Over the next ten years he suffered 3 more major losses, ending with his best friend, John, dying in his arms from swine flu. He hid his mental illness from everyone. He was the captain of the soccer team, the alpha male, accomplished architectural draftsman, well liked and had many girlfriends.

But beneath his facade of happy go lucky party boy, there were cracks and a darkness growing within. After John's death he was stricken with a serious illness, got into a very bad relationship with a girl who bled him dry emotionally and financially and bullied him to the point of suicide. I lost my son on the 20th March 2012, at the age of 27.

It was a tragic waste of a young life. He took his own life but didn't leave me suffering over the reason, leaving his will, eulogy and goodbye letters to his family and friends. His loss caused many adverse reactions like dropping a stone into a pool the ripples travel far and wide. His friends, work and teammates needed counselling for their shock. Our family relationships broke down and we were drowning in grief and guilt, eaten up alive with the "what ifs" and "maybes". I didn't lose one child I lost three. My family couldn't handle my grief and the loss of my own mental health. The shock of what I saw sent me into darkness. I developed PTSD and depression. I was lost and suicidal.

But realizing I needed help I sought out counselling from psychologists, support groups, compassionate friends, and bereavement counsellor and took medication.

I needed something positive to come out of his loss. So I started campaigning for mental health awareness, volunteering for mental health organizations, going to the media, fundraising for these organizations and for the past 7 years I have been giving mental health presentations at high schools to thousands of students. This is my son's legacy and my way of honouring his memory. There is a poem I read out at every presentation:

"I will be your legacy, I will be your voice.
You live on in me, so I have made the choice
to honour your life, by living again.
I love you, I miss you, and I will see you again

ERIF WADE
1.11.1984 to 21.2.2015

Erif, my daughter, was my first born, conceived after 11 years of marriage when I had given up hope of ever becoming pregnant. She arrived in the world on 1st November (All Saints' Day) 1984 and was a beautiful, happy and bright child.

She excelled at school, was very popular, and loved sports. She belonged to the local swimming club and took part in judo and gymnastics. She also had a nice singing voice (she was part of her school choir) and an artistic streak (neither inherited from me).

I worked part time when she was growing up, so I had time to spend with her and her younger brother born in 1986.

Everything changed when she was 10. The company I worked for was sold and I was told I could have a job for 2 years, but it had to be full time and I had to train for something else - so I suddenly was very busy and much stressed. At the same time, I had to find a full-time child-minder and, unknown to me, my daughter started being abused by the son of a neighbour. I never knew about this when she was growing up; he threatened to hurt her pets and he used physical violence to keep her quiet. I am full of self-blame that I didn't know and was just too busy to notice.

She did start to have mood swings, but I thought it was part of growing up and she was very good at hiding what was going on. However, she still had many friends and got good GCSE and A levels and things were not too bad until she went to University. She went a long way away - to Kent - which hurt at the time but apparently, it was to get away from him. He only abused her for a couple of years, but she was still terrified of him.

She got a good degree (2005) and met a nice boy but then she asked me to visit and told me she had developed a problem with alcohol, and she had to get a detox. I don't think any of us realised how serious it was, she was drinking a lot but seemed to have it under control. We very naively thought that the detox would solve all the problems. After the detox she went back to Kent with her boyfriend intending to get a job there. However, she started drinking again, much more heavily and they argued and split up, so she came home.

By 2007, she was very ill, she was hardly eating, drinking a lot and having withdrawal seizures and we were getting very little help. When she had a seizure, we called an ambulance. They would take her to hospital, keep her in for a few days while they gave her detox medication and then release her, and the cycle began again. So, we decided we would pay for private rehab - I really believed she would die without it. She was there for 3 months and the change was wonderful – I got my loving, sensitive, caring, beautiful, bright daughter back again.

She decided to stay in the same town as the rehab facility because they offered her a part time job helping there. For 3-4 months, everything was fine but then she started drinking again and came back home. We could not afford to pay for another private rehab and again we got no help from the NHS. We paid for some private counselling but that didn't seem to help. She also started to have seizures again and these were getting progressively more violent.

In 2009, she was arrested and subsequently put on probation. This also coincided with a particularly bad set of seizures and, in hospital, the doctor told her that the next set would probably kill her. The probation lady was wonderful and her help, together with Erif's terror of more seizures seemed to work a miracle. In 2010, she stopped drinking, she got a job she loved, started to eat healthily and she re-met a boy she had known in high school. She also started a counselling course so that she could make use of her degree. She and I built a really close relationship again and shared many things together including discovering a love of geocaching which gave us many adventures. During this time, she was a true friend as well as a beloved daughter.

She would not talk much about the abuse except to say that she wanted to forget it and did not want to try and pursue charges – I think she was still afraid of him – and it seemed best just to try and move on. In early 2012, she and her boyfriend moved in together and in late 2012, they decided to have a baby. She got pregnant straight away and Warren was born in late April 2013.

Unfortunately, she had a very bad time giving birth. She still had a lot of body issues and that, combined with an incompetent midwife, caused huge trauma. Fortunately, everything was OK in the end although Erif and the baby (who was quite poorly mainly because of the mishandling of Erif's labour) had to spend the first two weeks of his life in hospital. We did put a complaint into the hospital but never really got a satisfactory response.

The experience left a mark on Erif and she suffered from post-natal depression. At the beginning of 2014, she started drinking again. Not continuously but every 3-4 months she would have a binge which lasted a couple of days. Each time she said it was the last time. I asked to work part-time so I could support her, and we helped her as much as we could.

Most of the time, she was fine, but we never knew what would trigger her. When she was not drinking, she was a wonderful mother and she never actually drank when she was with her baby, it was only on days when he stayed with us or his other grandparents. In October 2014, she had a particularly bad binge and child services got involved. However, after that, things improved. Erif started an alcohol awareness course, started attending AA again and volunteered at a local pet rescue centre. Social Services said they were happy and signed her off. Everything seemed positive and Erif appeared happy.

On the weekend of February 14th 2015, Erif, her partner and the baby stayed at my house and Erif helped me out at a charity event. We put the baby to bed on the Saturday night and we all had a Valentine take-away. It was a good weekend; the last ever. On Monday Erif and I took Warren to a local indoor water park and had a great time and I baby sat in the evening whilst she went to AA and her partner went to Alanon (a support group for people who share lives with an alcoholic).

On the Thursday evening, she and Warren called round at my house on their way home but didn't stay long as she had another AA meeting to go to. I have been told she seemed to be happy at the meeting and had been asked to become treasurer which she was pleased about.

I have no idea why she started drinking again on the Friday (Feb 20th), but her partner came home and found she had been drinking (Warren was at his parents). They had a row and she stormed out. I do not know why he let her take the car keys – taking the keys off her was the first thing we ever did when she had been drinking in the past. We were frantically trying to find her, and she eventually called me at about 2 am. She said she was not sure where she was – I begged her not to drive, I said she should get a hotel for the night and I would pay, I even said I would come and get her. Unfortunately, her phone was low on battery and cut out.

The last thing she said was that she was going home. She sounded reasonably sober and, as it turned out, she was not that far over the drink/drive limit. I don't know and never will know what happened next. She had just passed a speed camera which was live, but she didn't trip it, so she wasn't speeding. It seems that she caught the car wheel on a high verge and the car turned over. She suffered head and neck injuries and died at the scene.

In spite of the years when she was drinking, I always loved her and always will. I tried so hard to protect her. She worked so hard at conquering her addiction. She loved her baby son so much. I miss her so very badly and would give anything for just one more day with her. I will miss her and love her as long as I live.

I can't remember that much of the first couple of years after Erif died. I felt that I had died also – or at least, I didn't want to carry on living. I spent long hours staring at nothing and thoughts would not stay in my head.

I couldn't eat and lost 3 stone. I couldn't bear to wear anything I had worn when she was alive, and I couldn't bear to go to any places I had been with her.

I found my husband's grief almost impossible to bear; it was as if it doubled mine and we were little comfort to each other. I spent a lot of time driving and parking up in quiet places where I could howl and scream.

I found it impossible to return to work. In an instant, a job which meant a great deal to me suddenly meant nothing and I knew I would no longer be able to cope with the pressures and the deadlines; I felt as if my mind had stopped working. They were good to me and gave me time off but in the end, I handed in my notice and walked away.

The first of Erif's birthdays after she died was especially hard. Her birthday is November 1st and I went into labour on 31st October, so Halloween and Bonfire night had always been part of the celebrations but that year (and in fact every year since) I have found them unbearable. I wrote this poem to express how I felt about Halloween.

All Hallows Eve is a holy day
Far holier than Eastertide or the Christ-child's birth.
Those twin commercial shams of holiness
This day was made holy by pain, and joy,
and pain so vast
It eclipsed the joy
I cannot share this day
I bar the door and shun the children in their gaudy cloths
I share this holy day with no-one
Except my own ghosts

There was no celebration of Christmas either; the decorations I boxed and put away in the loft in early January 2015 have remained untouched ever since. I sent no cards and bought no presents and gave money instead to charities supporting the homeless. This I have continued ever since, and I like to feel Erif would understand and approve.

The first anniversary was also very hard. I booked a room in a hotel just a very short distance down the road from where she died and asked for a room overlooking the road. Mark (my husband) slept but I sat up all night crying and staring out of the window with some foolish thought that I could see her drive by and stop her.

As I was near a complete breakdown, I had some counselling which helped, in that it gave me time and space to express my grief. However, the things that really helped me through those first two years, and since, have been The Compassionate Friends and Drugfam. I found The Compassionate Friends just after Erif's funeral when I was mindlessly searching my computer with some vague hope that I would find something to help and I stumbled across the TCF forum.

My first post was entitled 'Don't want to be here, don't want to be anywhere' and that summed up exactly how I felt. My post was answered by another grieving mother who had lost her son just three weeks before I lost Erif and was in as much grief and turmoil as I was. In those early days, she was the one person I could bear to be with, and she has remained a firm friend ever since.

I found Drugfam through their annual Bereavement Conference - I attended the first one the year Erif died. I was honoured to be asked to give a presentation of her story in 2016 and in 2017 I was invited to attend a Drugfam service in Westminster Abbey.

Nearly five years on, my grief is more manageable although the sadness never really goes and sometimes, especially around significant days, the ache becomes almost unbearable again. I had my precious girl for 30 years and I shall mourn her loss for much longer than that. I have struggled a little bit with the definition of legacy, partly because there are no big things which I have done such as set up a charity or a benefit in Erif's name.

I looked up some definitions of the word legacy and, amongst other things, I found this – "Remember, it's not what we leave FOR others that matters; it's what we leave IN them that matters most. Possessions and wealth do not a true legacy make. It's about leaving behind the essence of your Authentic Soul. A legacy isn't always about things. Usually, it's about who you are and how you touch people's lives".

So, if I look at it the other way round, I see that what is really important is the legacy Erif left to me and that is the memory of who she was, and her child – my grandson. My legacy to her is to help him to grow up to be the person she wanted him to be and to also know how very much she loved him. It has not been easy, no child should suffer such a devastating loss at such a young age (he was just coming up to 2) and it had, and still has, an effect on him.

He was just beginning to talk but he stopped, and he didn't begin to talk again until well over a year later. He is still very clingy, does not like to be left and has a lot of anxiety especially about fears of being abandoned. However, he is his mother's son, so he is bright and outgoing and has an empathy for others far beyond his years. I try my best to make him feel secure and loved and to give him all the experiences Erif would want him to have.

Also, I have collated books and memory boxes for him. These contain photos and videos of his time with his mum, letters to him from her friends and relatives describing their memories, letters she wrote to him and other writings she did when she was pregnant and Facebook posts about her pregnancy and the early days of his life journey – the intention is to make sure he has a record of their time together and to always know how much she loved him.

There are other things I have done in Erif's memory. I was asked to be a moderator on one of the TCF Facebook groups and I try to use that to reach out to other bereaved parents, especially those who have a similar story. As part of that, I pulled together a poetry book in 2016 from contributions from other bereaved parents.

I have always loved poetry and it seemed only natural that, after Erif's death, I should turn to poetry again to try and find some solace and this I did; weeping endless tears over such gems as Christina Rossetti's "Remember" and Lyman Hancock's "When I am Gone".

I can't remember now who from our Facebook group wrote the first poem or even the second one. I know the writing was accelerated after several of us attended a creative writing workshop at the first supportive weekend for those bereaved by substance abuse and suicide in 2016 at Woodbrook.

By the time of the Drugfam Bereaved by Addiction conference in October 2017, the number of poems (like Topsy) had grown considerably – most were written by mothers but some by fathers and siblings. Someone had the idea of putting them all together into a book and I, with the thought of Erif's birthday and then Christmas coming up and the need to distract myself from painful memories, offered to pull it together.

Most of the decisions about the book were made jointly by those who had contributed poems. The format we decided upon was to introduce each child with some information about them (significant dates, mother, fathers, siblings etc.) followed by a photograph and a shortish biography and then the poems.

The title of the book "They were So Much More: Expressions of Love and Grief" indicates how the contributors feel about our children and how special and loved they were (and still are of course) in spite of their problems.

In all it took well over 6 months even with a lot of help with suggestions, proof reading, etc. before we all had copies of our book. Although I was proud of how the book looked, its beauty was not in the page lay-outs or the format but in the poems, which are so full of our love for our children and our grief at the tragedy of their loss. Below are some quotes from people who have read the book:

"Such a beautiful book. Thank-you all for sharing your stories, thoughts and poems".

"It has really helped me to see your beautiful children. Even though my heart breaks for each and every one of us."
"All my friends love the book too and all of them cried. It is so beautiful and does make them all real."
"It is beautiful and the poems and stories so emotional but uplifting too. Such an amazing expression of love."
"These poems and shares are so poignant and loving – inspiring."
"Such a wonderful tribute to all our children."
"The poetry throughout the book is so raw, beautiful and heartfelt. I feel that I am beginning to know so much more about all the children we honour, what a wonderful tribute."
"This is a beautiful tribute to our children."

As well as personal copies for the contributors, several of the books were sold to raise money for The Compassionate Friends and Drugfam.

There are other things I have done in honour of Erif, but these are mainly very small things. I have set up a part of my garden where I have placed plants which have out-grown baskets and pots left by her friends on her grave – and there is a small oak tree there grown from an acorn I picked up from the roadside where she died.

Also, I have set up a geocache in her memory so that others enjoying this sport can think of her.

Maybe someday I will do more in her memory but, for now, her greatest legacy is the memory of her I carry in my heart.

VICKI MEAGHER
12.5.1982 to 13.11.2017

Vicki was born in the middle of the Falklands War, in 1982, and was followed by her brother Ben two years later. Their father was in the Royal Air Force, so we moved a few times when the children were very small, including spending three years in Germany, before settling in Oxfordshire when Vicki was five and Ben was three. Life was very normal, with Ben playing football for the local team and later on for the County, and Vicki spending several hours a week at the nearby dance school, learning ballet, tap, and modern dance to a very high standard. Vicki went to university in Twickenham, and then embarked on adult life, settling down in Witney with her boyfriend Chris, and working in a market research company based in Wallingford. In 2012, Vicki and

Chris had a daughter, Phoebe, and the following year they got married; surely the basis for happy ever after.

In June 2014, Vicki was diagnosed with breast cancer. For someone with a very healthy lifestyle and no family history of cancer, this came out of the blue and was a huge shock to all of us, but Vicki dealt with the diagnosis and the subsequent treatment with her characteristic courage and humour; she always insisted she was not 'fighting' cancer, but living with it. She had chemotherapy at the Churchill hospital in Oxford, and in December that year a mastectomy, followed by radiotherapy. In February 2015, she was declared cancer free, and we thought that life would go back to normal.

In December the same year Vicki had a routine follow-up appointment with her oncologist, and while she was with him, she mentioned a pain in her sternum that had persisted for a couple of months. He referred her for a scan to be on the safe side, and a week later, she went to the Churchill for the results. In Vicki's own words "When I came to the results appointment and saw the breast care nurse waiting with the oncologist, I knew. I knew what he was going to tell me and I began to shake." Vicki was diagnosed with incurable stage four cancer: she had been 'cancer free' for just 10 months.

Through the treatment that followed, the oncologist tried hard to balance Vicki's quality of life with quantity; Vicki herself said that she wanted quantity so that she could spend as long as possible with Phoebe. During this time, she attended a support group run by the charity Breast Cancer Care at the Maggie's Centre in Oxford, and became an ambassador for BCC's 'Secondary not Second Rate' campaign, featuring in several videos to raise awareness of the difficulties faced by women with incurable breast cancer; highlighting for example that 72% of hospital organisations in England, Scotland and Wales don't give patients access to a dedicated secondary breast care nurse. She also wrote articles for BCC to publicise the campaign – the quote above is taken from a feature published in Huffington Post.

In summer 2016, Ben decided that he wanted to use his lifetime experience of football playing to raise funds for cancer charities, and organised a world record attempt in Wales, where he lives with his wife Lucie. The attempt was titled Kicking Off Against Cancer, and the record was ratified some time later by Guinness World Records– the team was the official holder of the longest ever indoor six-a-side football match, having played non-stop for 36 hours.

Vicki died in November 2017 and in the following year, friends and family raised money for Breast Cancer Care and Maggie's Centres in her name, contributing over £10,000 from walking a half marathon and other events. Ben and Lucie decided to use the experience they had gained from running the world record attempt to set up a registered charity, also called Kicking Off Against Cancer, which is now a thriving organisation providing help and support for people living with cancer, and helping them make memories with the people closest to them. As well as arranging days out and weekends away for families, KOAC has donated toys and games to a local children's hospital, and arranged hospitality trips to concerts and sporting events. In July 2019, the trustees decided that it was time to attempt another world record, and this time played 11 a-side football for a staggering 169 hours, or one week and one hour, beating the previous record by that one extra hour, and raising almost £25,000 to continue KOACs work, inspired by Vicki's legacy of extraordinary courage in dealing with her illness. At the time of writing, we're waiting to hear if Guinness will confirm that the KOAC team is the official world record holder.

Phoebe is a focus for the whole family, with all of us helping her Dad, Chris, to deal with being a single parent, covering time in the school holidays and making sure he gets some down time to be with friends. Phoebe is very like her mother, and surely the best legacy Vicki could have left behind.

Despite the great joy that Phoebe brings me, life without my daughter is very hard in so many different ways, from the purely practical to the emotional incidents that can ambush me with no warning on an otherwise 'normal' day. We used to text each other frequently, and I still sometimes find myself picking up my phone to tell her something; remembering each time all over again that she isn't here. I've learnt the hard way that I need to be with other people on key dates like New Year's Eve and Vicki's birthday, in order to get through those events. When I broke a bone in my foot recently and needed help to get home from the local A&E Unit on crutches and with my foot in plaster, I was very aware that it would have been Vicki I would have called for help in the past, and although some very lovely friends helped out, I missed her as much then as when she first died. The weeks leading up to the anniversary of her death are particularly difficult, as I go over in my mind the events that happened on each day.

When Vicki died, the company I was working for gave me five days 'compassionate' leave, something which I have felt strongly ever since was not compassionate at all. I took another five days unpaid, which financially I couldn't afford, but emotionally had to do. Although the corporate response to my grief was so harsh, my family and friends were, and continue to be, amazingly supportive, and I will always be grateful for their care and encouragement.

Vicki made me laugh; when we played Pictionary, we weren't allowed to be on the same team as we always knew straight away what the other was drawing. When she was a little girl and made me cards for special occasions, she used to draw a bar code on the back. Her bedroom was always a mess, and when she was old enough, she loved getting tattoos. She was enormously well organised as an adult, and ran the family by making lists; our mantra was 'what's the plan?' We liked a lot of the same books and made TV recommendations: Strictly and the Bake Off are hard for me to watch without her. She was the bravest person that I have ever known, and she made no concessions to cancer.

We were lucky in that the illness didn't impact her life in terms of pain or weakness until relatively soon before she died, and she continued to work, around her treatment plan, until a month before she was admitted to hospital for the last time. It was her major preoccupation to keep the routine as normal as possible for Phoebe, and she and Chris succeeded in this right up to the end of Vicki's life. She always said that she didn't want a big funeral, but that we should organise a party in her memory instead. Chris and Ben arranged this six weeks after her death, and I was immeasurably touched by the amount of people who came to pay tribute to her; from her closest friends and work colleagues, to mums she knew from the school gate, family, friends from her BCC Group and a Facebook cancer support site she had been a part of; Vicki made a lasting impact on all who met her, and despite missing her so desperately, I feel honoured and grateful that we had her with us for 35 years.

LUCY REBECCA CURRAN
23.10.2001 to 14.2.2018

On 23rd October 2001 Lucy Rebecca Curran shot into this world only about an hour after I went into labour. My husband Mark and I barely made it to the hospital in time. The birth of my son, Andrew, the year before, had been quick so we had suspected this might be the case but little did we know this bundle of energy would arrive at top speed, cram so much living into the next sixteen years and then tragically depart this world as quickly as she arrived.

Lucy was one of life's characters. When you first met Lucy, she would come across as being polite and quite shy but as soon as you got to know her you would realise she was excitable, had the most beautiful smile and the most contagious of laughs.

She discovered one of her passions at the age of 2 when she joined the Glenda Egan School of Dance. She danced there for the rest of her life and we were always very surprised that someone as clumsy as Lucy (she would frequently fall over her own feet!) could become such a beautiful dancer. As she got older she also loved to choreograph with her friends. My home would become a dance studio on a Saturday afternoon as the girls loved to come back from dance class and take over the living room or the garden patio to make up dances for the annual show.

Her other passion was music and it was through music she learnt the rewards of hard work. The first instrument she played was the clarinet; however at the age of 10, she was reluctant to practice as much as she should and this led to a very mediocre report from her music teacher. Lucy was not happy with the report and over the next twelve months put in a lot of time and effort and received a glowing report the following year. She went on to learn to play the piano, taught herself the ukulele and then decided to start learning the guitar.

Not only did she like to play music but she also loved nothing more than following bands and going to gigs. She had a diverse taste in music and was a familiar face at many of the Glasgow music venues. My best friend since school (also Lucy's godmother), Nicki, and I still love our music and gigs so I do think we were in part responsible for this obsession!

Lucy and I shared lots of interests including travel. As a family we were lucky enough to travel to all sorts of exciting places such as Australia, Hong Kong, Egypt, USA, France, Austria and Germany. We are not well off and always travelled on a budget but I am so glad we made the effort and Lucy was able to see so many wonderful places and meet many interesting people. Lucy and I were planning a trip to Kenya to visit Evaline, a young girl we have sponsored as a family for many years, but sadly we never got to make this trip.

Lucy would have loved seeing the wildlife in Africa as she loved animals. She grew up with Nicki's dog Bear. Funnily enough they were the same age and Lucy would spend hours fussing over Bear who was a gentle giant, being a Newfoundland/Collie cross. I am convinced her love of animals was thanks to Bear. I have the most wonderful memory of Lucy as a toddler lying underneath the rather large Bear, tickling his tummy while giggling with glee! Lucy was delighted to get her first pet rabbit at the age of 10 and a couple of years later in true Lucy fashion she persuaded me, with the help of a Power Point presentation, to get our dog Rosie. It is fair to say that Lucy doted on Rosie and insisted on having a proper birthday party on her first birthday complete with doggie birthday cake and a rendition of "Happy Birthday to you"!

When Lucy reached her teenage years she became an advocate for equality in all walks of life. This was reinforced by the sign on her bedroom door which advised you were not to enter if you were racist, sexist, ablest, homophobic….the list was endless. She really influenced people not to be judgemental of others which makes me very proud.

I was blessed to have a very close relationship with Lucy and we shared a lot of the same interests and could speak to each other about anything. Now don't get me wrong Lucy did have some "teenage moments" but don't we all – I am in my late forties and still have my moments!

I am also lucky to have a good relationship with Lucy's many friends. When Lucy and her friends discovered a new local band at the age of fourteen they asked me to go along with them to the gig as the responsible adult. This turned out to be one of my better decisions as the band in question are called Single by Sunday and Lucy ended up becoming close friends with them and their families and a huge fan of their music.

On the surface Lucy came across as being carefree however she was one of life's worriers. I think it stemmed from a desire to please people and not let anyone down. This was particularly apparent in the school environment and although we did not put pressure on her she never wanted to let her teachers down. The school was one of the highest performing schools in the country and put immense pressure on the young people to do well academically.

Lucy worked hard and got good results but always felt she should be doing better. Her issues with exam stress became apparent in the run up to the National 5 exams and she was struggling to sleep and was getting increasingly anxious.

We went to the GP and, as there were no counselling options available in the immediate future, Lucy was prescribed a tablet to take not every day but as and when required. I was concerned about going down the medication route but was assured this was a mild, non-addictive beta blocker and when I looked into it, I found quite a few friends and family members had taken this in the past. As a result Lucy did become calmer and did very well in her exams.

It wasn't until the run up to her higher exams the following year that she felt the need to take the tablets again. It was the night before her prelims and she was nervous about the upcoming exams. Unbeknown to me she had taken a tablet, felt it was making no difference and made the fateful decision to take some more. In her head she was thinking of the doctor saying take them "as and when required" and in her anxious state had thought this was a time she very much needed them. She did not realise she had done anything wrong and it was not until she started feeling poorly that she mentioned to me she had taken them. She pulled on some clothes over her pyjamas as I frantically dialled 999 and called for Mark and Andrew to come. She very quickly deteriorated and lost consciousness. I went in the ambulance with her to the hospital and the beta blockers basically stopped her heart and suddenly there I was holding my precious child's hand as she slipped away from this world on 14th February 2018. As I write these words I still can't quite believe it.

However isn't it poignant that Lucy, who loved and was loved by so many, left us on the day of love, St Valentine's Day.

In the immediate aftermath it was utter shock like an out of body experience, happening to someone else. The next couple of weeks were filled with constant visitors and the heart-breaking task of planning the funeral. To this day I am still overwhelmed at the kindness shown to us from so many. Seeing almost five hundred people squeezed into the church and church hall at Lucy's memorial service gave us a glimpse of just how popular Lucy was with so many.

I always knew Lucy to be kind and caring of others however we left cards out at her funeral and asked people to write a memory of Lucy on them and I learnt so much more about my beautiful girl. Although she was not her happiest at school there were several stories from girls in some of her classes who said no one spoke to them apart from Lucy. She would approach them at first asking what kind of music and bands they liked and strike up a conversation the best way she knew through music. I want to share with you the beautiful tribute her close friend Helen wrote for the school yearbook.

"Summing Lucy up in just a few words would be a massive disservice to her. Although she was kind, sweet and caring she was also so much more than that. She loved music and going to concerts and talking about bands. Although sometimes her taste was questionable. She enjoyed playing many different instruments including the piano and clarinet. Lucy loved to dance, every chance she got she was up having a boogie whether it be in her living room or performing on stage with her dance group. She was a great animal lover, being the proud owner of Sootie the rabbit and Rosie her dog. Lucy was someone you could cry with one minute and laugh with the next. She would put other people's needs before her own and always be there when you needed her. You could talk to her about anything, nothing was off limits and so many conversations would end with her contagious laugh. Although she may no longer be with us, she will always be part of our year group and stay with us in our memories."

The day after Lucy's funeral the worst snow we have had for years arrived so the visitors could come no more and the stark reality of our loss came to the fore. Over the next couple of days I had some terrible thoughts – the thought of life without Lucy was inconceivable but I had my son Andrew and Lucy's dog Rosie who needed me so that was that.

Also the kindness that had been shown by Lucy's friends in particular overwhelmed me. Every group of her friends came to see me although they were so lost and they keep in touch to this day. Their friendship means so much to me. They have been so acutely affected by their loss that I take great solace from seeing how special Lucy remains to them.

As someone who is not on social media, I will forever be grateful to my niece Amy for showing me Lucy's page on twitter – I was totally unaware that Lucy used to post tweets about me. I get so much comfort from her sharing things like "Guys OMG my mum is amazing", "Can't even begin to explain how much I love my mum", "Still so proud of my mum for all the charity work she did in Peru" and "When you get a text from your mum to say she just snuck into a concert....I knew I was related to that woman". But there were two recent ones which struck a chord "I love music so much" and "I want to do something with my life."

I decided Lucy was on this earth and touched so many hearts for a reason so I set up Lucy's Memorial Fund which would benefit the music therapy charity Nordoff Robbins. Lucy had an involvement with them through her favourite band and would always make me tick the box to donate to them when booking concert tickets! I met with the charity and before we knew it the first event was being planned by Single by Sunday – a memorial gig at one of the music venues in Glasgow which was to include a performance from her dance class, two of her favourite bands as support and Single by Sunday to headline. Very early on I realised that the focus and planning of an event in Lucy's memory helped me so much. It was an emotional and amazing night – the perfect tribute to Lucy.

As soon as the gig was over I made the decision to go back to work and my wonderful friends at work suggested we run the next event for Lucy's memorial – an open mic/karaoke night. At the work event I had an unusual experience and our guest speaker from Nordoff Robbins showed a short video of a severely autistic child responding to her parents for the first time after six months of music therapy. I swear Lucy was over my shoulder saying, "Mum you are doing the right thing. Keep going with it."

After just 2 events Lucy's Memorial Fund had reached almost £5,000. I was so proud that because of Lucy so many vulnerable children and adults would benefit. Her legacy of helping others through music was well underway.

I think it helped Andrew to become involved too. He has always been a bit of a daredevil and chose to do a sky dive in memory of his little sister. My heart was in my mouth as he hurtled from 10,000 feet in the air but he loved every moment of it and raised over £1,000 for Lucy's Memorial Fund.

The next event I planned was a 5k walk/run for females called the "Race for Luce". I was amazed that over 130 girls signed up and on a Sunday morning in late September we all wore our special t-shirts for Lucy and completed the 5k and then went back to the church hall for refreshments. Friends in Australia and Canada also participated so the race went global! Events like this take a lot of work and I have the most wonderful support network and so many people took their part in helping organise the event and Lucy was the central focus which was so special. It was such a success we repeated the race again the following year.

Now don't get me wrong, the positive focus of Lucy's Memorial Fund really helps but I need to do this alongside my grieving. When I take Rosie on her morning walk every day that is my "Lucy Time" when I listen to her music, talk to her, cry and smile at some of the precious memories.

Lucy and I always planned to do a charity trek along part of the Great Wall of China when she was eighteen so the next event was obvious to me. In 2019 the year she would have turned eighteen my friend Jenny who lives in Australia met me in Beijing and we did that trek for Lucy. Not only did this raise a lot of money for Nordoff Robbins but it made me realise that walking helps so I have decided to try and do a walk for Lucy each year. I have signed up to walk through part of the Jordanian desert to Petra next. The planning and training keeps me busy and meeting new people and talking to them about Lucy is a comfort. Lucy asked me once if I hadn't had her and Andrew what would I have done to which I answered I would have travelled more. She also loved to travel so I have arranged quite a few travels for next year. Lucy, of course, will travel with me and I now leave a "lovelock" with a special message to her each place I go.

Her legacy goes further than just her Memorial Fund. Her dance school dedicated the annual dance show to Lucy in 2018 and that evening they announced they were setting up the Lucy Curran Awards. I was honoured and very proud to present the junior, intermediate and senior trophies at the dance show this year.

Mark's football team also played in the Lucy Curran Memorial League Cup and invited me along to present the trophy. Any event which remembers Lucy means the world to us.

I am delighted to say that Lucy's Memorial fund has already raised in excess of £11,000 and we are now planning our biggest event to date, "Lucyfest." This will be a charity gig at the Barrowlands, an iconic Glasgow music venue and also one of Lucy's favourite places.

It's not my choice but I have been forced into mothering both my children in different ways. Andrew and Lucy will always be the most important people in my life. I will continue to enjoy my time with Andrew and carry on his parenting in the conventional sense and I will strive to keep Lucy's memory alive and include her in everything I do. Whether I am presenting the Lucy Curran Awards or organising something to raise money for Lucy's Memorial Fund I feel immensely proud of Lucy herself and of her legacy of helping others through music.

It is said the brightest lights shine the shortest and this very much sums up Lucy.

WILL HOUGHTON
24.7.1995 to 29.1.2016

Will Houghton was living his best life when his world stopped. In 2016 the super-fit twenty year old was flying through the Hampshire countryside on his bicycle when he was knocked down by a car. He died of his injuries.

At the Houghton's house in Buckinghamshire a tall and handsome Will smiles out of family portraits. The bright red racing bike he bought but never rode – it arrived a fortnight after his death – hangs on a wall.

Liz Houghton, his mother, recalls how she would come downstairs in the morning to find him sitting red-faced and muddy in the kitchen, having cycled 50 miles before breakfast: "He would be stuffing his face with porridge and saying 'we live in such a beautiful country Mum'. "That's what cycling gave him". Will, head boy at his school, Claire's Court, Maidenhead, had a strong sense of justice, wanted to help the disadvantaged and was sharply aware of how fortunate his own life was. His dream was to be the next Bradley Wiggins as his lively sports science studies demonstrated at Portsmouth University together with his love of US politics, reality TV and skittles.

She remembers the January day when her life changed irrevocably. She was at work when she had a call from her husband Richard saying Will had been knocked off his bike. She expected bad grazes but he said "no, it's serious". The police sent a car for them and it was blue-lighted all the way to Southampton Hospital, the whole journey Liz thinking it might be touch and go but as he was so fit and healthy he should pull through it. She even thought of campaigning for more cycle paths to prevent similar accidents as the car sped to their destination.

Then the devastating reality of it all kicked in with the doctor's words "it's unsurvivable". The impact had killed Will immediately, going over the top of an elderly woman's car and hitting the back of his head on the road. The driver didn't even see him.

"I remember this sound coming out of my mouth; this awful noise and realising I was making it" recalls Liz. Even while trying to process this devastating news she knew what Will would have wanted, telling the nurse they must save all his organs as he'd had a donor card since he was 18. "I think because he knew it was dangerous riding a bike on the road he'd made preparations in case the worst happened" muses Liz. They said goodbye to Will, she took photos of him, his lovely brown eyes and spoke to him: "Oh Will, how can this be? Why aren't you here" Trying to rationalise the events and leaving him there she found horrendous.

"The nurses were wonderful, the NHS outstanding, but I was at a loss. Everyone was carrying on with their lives and our son had died. But just because Will is not here it doesn't mean my emotional relationship with him has ended. I am still his mother. I always will be. What scares me most is that I'll lose my memories of him" she cries.

Liz knew Will would want to make a difference; that his death would help save lives, the ultimate gift. She knew it would mean so much to the whole family to know he would be helping make other people's lives better, giving them some kind of solace.

For this reason, Liz, founder of the women's clothing chain Mint Velvet, has launched a new initiative, "Don't Forget the Donor", in conjunction with NHS Blood and Transplant which helps organ recipients to write anonymously – when and if they feel able – to the bereaved ones of donors.

She knows the process of writing can, for many, be fraught with difficulties, feeling their words will seem inadequate, even ill-judged. "They are frightened of offending - no one wants to talk about grief – and they don't know what to say" Liz says. "They worry about re-opening old wounds but I'm never going to forget my son died am I? Just a few simple sentences make all the difference and this initiative is about informing and educating".

Ninety percent of donor families wish to hear from recipients but fewer than twenty percent receive any acknowledgement. All they get is a factual up-date from the NHS. Through these short bulletins Liz has learned that Will's eyes have helped four people to see; that his heart beats in another man's chest; that his bones and skin have been processed and stored for grafting. She knows too, that one of his kidneys has allowed a father in his 50's to come off of dialysis; that part of Will's liver has saved the life of a desperately ill child.

"There are probably about twelve people who have already benefited from different parts of Will's body", says Liz "but of these, just two families have contacted us". One, from a mother of a young child debilitated by a rare liver disease who received Will's healthy liver recounts: "This letter is the hardest I have ever had to write because I'm trying to put into words how grateful I am". She compared the perilous state of her young son's health to balancing on a cliff edge on one leg waiting for a sharp gust of wind to throw him off the edge. She had lived in that state for three years.

Then came Will's precious gift. "Your son is our hero and part of him will always live on in my son's life" she wrote. "I think about Will every day. He must have been an inspiration".

Liz cherishes this letter; "It made me feel so wonderful. I sent her photos of Will and a reply. I wanted her to know that sending her letter was the very best thing she could have done. She says a little prayer for Will every night and I love thinking about that. I wrote to her how pleased I was and how her letter means everything to me".

"I'd say to other donors' families: if you get a letter please acknowledge it for it then becomes a circle of gratitude".

The other letter was from a son whose father had been on dialysis for more than ten years and had been distraught with grief at being too sick to fly to his mother's funeral abroad. Will's kidney had transformed his life.

"One of the first things he did when he was well enough" wrote his son, "was to fly and visit her grave and pay his respects. My father is forever grateful for that". Such details lift Liz. "What do you say to the mother of a son who died yet managed to save my father's life?" the young man went on in his letter. "Thank you just doesn't seem enough but that is all I can offer. Thank you for bringing such a brave and selfless individual into this world. Without him my father would not be here now. Thank you for Will".

Liz, 54, is determined to wring something positive from the "senseless" tragedy of her son's death. Endlessly resourceful, she works continually but tears often blur her eyes. A forthright woman of warmth and kindness, she is conscious too of the need to maintain a façade of cheerfulness for the family's sake.

She and her husband Richard, 55, who runs a PR consultancy, have two other children, Tom, 23, just 13 months Will's junior and Sophie 18. At their handsome Arts and Crafts era home in Buckinghamshire, set in landscaped gardens, all is tasteful and calm. Will, who was in his second year at university, is still present in photos that depict him on his bike, water skiing, larking about with his siblings and parents and hugging his beloved "Ooma" (grandma).

"When I'm on my own" continues Liz, "perhaps in the car, I think about how much I miss Will and it's like drowning so you have to stop yourself and come up for air. It is like a physical pressure, an overwhelming pain in your heart and for the first two or three years it's so acute it feels as if your heart will actually break so what I try to do is be positive: Will died. He is not coming back so I can either make the best of it or wallow in self-pity".

Turning back to the vital importance of the letters from donor recipients, Angie Ditchfield is one of a team of 250 specialist organ donor nurses around the country who liaises with Liz on the "Don't Forget the Donor" legacy. The nurses advocate for donor families, acting as intermediaries between them and recipients. There is no direct contact, both parties remaining anonymous.

"I think some recipients are scared that they might have to meet or end up on a TV show but that's not what I want" says Liz. "Some recipients are still very unwell. There can be complications. Sometimes organs can be rejected. Not everyone wants to write but if they do there should be someone saying: 'It's important. We'll help you'".

Angie adds: "What we're doing is supporting those recipients who want to communicate but may be daunted by the prospect of writing. Some think thank you is not enough yet that's all it takes. A letter is never going to take away the loss and grief but it often helps. At the very worst time in their lives they have thought of other people who are suffering and that selflessness is amazing".

Katie Morley, a recipient coordinator for NHS Blood and Transplant says it is important to remember that recipients should not feel pressured into writing as they may be dealing with physical and mental problems following surgery. Also not every transplant has a happy ending: two of Will's organs failed. "Transplant is a procedure that will hopefully lead to a better quality of life" Katie says, "but the recipients still have health problems. The drugs prescribed, for instance, often cause hand tremors which could make it difficult to write. Some medications can affect mood and heighten emotions during a period that is already emotional. Choosing whether or not to correspond with the donor families should not be forced onto anyone" concludes Katie.

The law is now changing in England and Scotland – but not Northern Ireland – from an opt-in to an opt-out system (it already applies in Wales). More than 6,200 Britons are waiting for life-saving transplants in the UK but on average three of them die each day.

Campaigners and medical professionals have long argued that having to actively register your consent has restricted the supply of organs. Up until now roughly two-thirds of families approached about donation agree: NHS BT aims for a consent rate of 80%. Wales has the highest consent rate of UK nations at 77%, up from 58% in 2015 when the law changed there but even so only 1% of people die in circumstances (such as a hospital intensive care unit or emergency department) that make it possible for them to be donors.

Angie Ditchfield thinks publicity around the change in the law will encourage people to have a conversation. "I think, as a society, we don't like talking about death and dying. Tell your loved ones what you want".

Liz, meanwhile, has written her own letter to all those Will has helped. It is on the NHS communication hub, there for all to see. She writes: "Will was our first born and from the minute he arrived was a joy in our lives".

"Every night when I go to bed I'm in that hospital again saying goodbye to Will. I think about his lungs. He had brilliant lung capacity. I wonder where they are now. He cared about other people and I know he'd be asking 'Mum, do you know who's got my heart? Do they know how fit I was?'"

Today Liz says: "It's as if I live in two worlds; part of me thinks it never happened, that Will is just away at university, because how on earth can someone who had so much to give suddenly not be here? It's unbelievable".

"People worry about upsetting me but I want to talk. I want to hear from Will's recipients. It's what keeps him present and his spirit alive". And what also keeps Will's memory alive is the Will Houghton Foundation which has been set up to work with UK charities to help 14-24 year olds to reach their potential through education and sport.

VICTORIA VOWLES
14.4.1980 to 8.9.2016

The day Victoria was born, changed my life. I felt complete as a woman and as a mother. I had always felt something was missing, but that gap was now filled with this perfect little person. I knew it was going to be hard, Victoria was my third pregnancy, my second to full term, but my husband had walked away before I'd realised I was expecting another child to accompany my then toddler son.

The birth itself was difficult, but when she arrived she was so beautiful, like a little doll with masses of black hair. She had to be whisked away to an incubator for a few hours as she was blue, due to the two hours of pushing and the labour stopping, but eventually she was allowed back to be with me. I wouldn't let her out my sight after that, she was so precious and the nurses showed me how to suck the fluid out her lungs, so I could do it myself. Her big brother, then 3 1/2 was brought to the hospital in the afternoon and seemed equally delighted with his little sister. I sat him on my bed and placed the new baby gently in his arms, his face beamed as he said "That's my new baby sister". It was indeed.

I'd travelled to stay with family late in the pregnancy as there was no-one to look after my son when I went into hospital; I stayed for a month after Victoria's birth to help me adjust and then returned to my little Kent cottage. We were a complete little unit, me and my two children.

Victoria was an extremely contented baby and rarely cried, I breastfed her for eighteen months and seemed to instinctively know when she was hungry. There seemed to be some sort of bond between us, which I hadn't felt before. She was very petite, which caused the health visitor to frequently visit me voicing her concern. I, however, was not concerned, she was putting on weight, extremely happy and seemed to love life. I explained that she was never going to be big as I wasn't and my mother had faced the same issues when I was little. It came to a head one day when the health visitor turned up while I was cooking Victoria's lunch of plaice cooked in goats milk, potatoes and vegetables. She seemed pleased with the food, but showed me a graph she'd prepared and proceeded to tell me that she felt Victoria had "lost her survival instinct". I was horrified. Victoria was about 18 months and was standing in the kitchen laughing. I asked her if that looked like a child that had lost her survival instinct.

I realised that as I was on my own with two children, living in a house that was in desperate need of repair, they needed to keep an eye on me, but this was ridiculous. She didn't come back and we got on with our lives.

Just before Victoria was 5, she was meant to start school, but she had gone down with whooping cough. We had had several months of illness....mumps, measles, chicken pox, German measles. The family doctor had advised against immunisation due to my ex-husband having a couple of epileptic episodes, so each illness had to be closely monitored by myself, making sure I closed the curtains when they got measles, to prevent eye damage. They survived and Victoria followed her big brother to school. On her first day the Headmaster lifted her up on his shoulder and introduced her to the other children; she was delighted.

She got on well at school, although one of her teachers told me "she's not like her brother is she?" Her brother was very placid, but Victoria was more of a 'doing' child. A typical example was, I sent them both into the garden one summer's day with a bucket and spade. Victoria started digging and making mud pies, her brother had upturned his bucket and was sat on it reading a book.

There are so many memories that spring to mind, she seemed to have a way with animals. When she was a teenager, a friend of hers had a horse that she couldn't seem to do anything with, she asked Victoria to go along to help and I was told later by the friend that Victoria had been like a 'Horse Whisperer'. Animals seemed to be drawn to her and she originally wanted to become a veterinary nurse, but then got interested in philosophy, which she later studied at University to Masters Level.

Victoria had a sense of humour and could sometimes be a little mischievous.

One day when she was at school her and a friend decided to get out of a PE lesson by Victoria faking an asthma attack. She did however go on to play rugby for Cheltenham and was very keen on keep fit and health.

But now I want my daughter to be here, but she's not, so the only way I can trick my mind into thinking she's still here....in part anyway....is to do something in which she lives on. Death changes everything, but time doesn't always move forward....or heal.

In the summer of 2016, I was suffering with shingles. I'd had a rough three or four years. At the end of 2012, I'd given up my two jobs and moved from Lincoln to London to look after my mother whose health was deteriorating. Unfortunately in March 2013, the inevitable happened and my mother died.

I found it emotionally exhausting trying to do everything on my own, although I should have been used to it, as I'd been doing everything on my own for very many years, but this was different, I was mourning the death of my mother, my father having died several years previously. I had to choose what clothes she was to wear in her coffin...this was after all, for eternity so had to be chosen well. I knew that no matter what, she had to have a Rosary in her hands.

The sorting of the various bags of paperwork that had accumulated over the years was hard, what I needed to keep, what could be shredded? Everyone had to be informed, arrangements made and the family home sold to pay inheritance tax. I found this extremely hard.

In 2014, the family home was ready to be sold and the tax man took his chunk of my parents' hard-earned home. I sold my house in Lincoln and moved back to the South East, into rented accommodation while I looked for a house to purchase. I rented a tiny bungalow and what wouldn't fit in, went into storage. My daughter, Victoria, got married in August and I spent six months frantically looking for a home, which I eventually found in February 2015, with a wonderful view of the South Downs.

Fast forward to the summer of 2016 and the strain of the last three years had taken its toll and I went down with shingles.

Victoria was expecting her first child in September and we had both discussed the fact that I needed to stay away, as although she had had chicken pox as a child, we were not going to take any chances. She was living in Gloucestershire and I was in East Sussex....so no popping round and as I was on very strong pain killers I was unable to drive, so that made it easier. We kept in contact over the phone and everything was progressing well with her pregnancy.

Late in the evening of the 7th September I experienced chest pain that felt different to the shingles pain I had been experiencing, so decided to go to bed, but the pain continued to such an extent that I wondered if I should call 111, the non-emergency number, to get advice.

I lay there for ages contemplating, when my mobile rang, displaying my daughter's name. As it was now in the early hours of a Thursday morning, I assumed she had either just had the baby, or was in labour. When I answered, a male voice on the other end said "Vickie's had a heart attack and they can't stop the bleeding".

My brain desperately tried to process what I had just heard....was this some kind of sick joke? Surely no-one would be that cruel. I gradually began to realise that it was my son-in-law and he was in shock. I asked him about the baby and he replied the baby was in intensive care. The baby had in fact been rushed to Bristol hospital, packed in ice and put on life support. I asked if his parents were with him (he was going to need them). He replied they were on their way.

I heard bells going off in the background and he said he had to go. I put the phone down and sat on my bed rocking backwards and forwards.

I prayed so hard to God that night...."Take me, take me, please don't take her, take me".

My mobile rang an hour later, still showing her name...I knew it was from my son-in-law. His words cut through the stillness of the night like an axe: "I'm so sorry".

That was three and a half years ago and life moves on. My little Granddaughter survived but the ripple effect of losing a child has not. It affected Victoria's husband of only two years and his parents who regarded Victoria as the daughter they didn't have, also siblings, friends; everyone that knew her and of course me, her mother.

After the initial inquest, I asked one of the surgeons who had tried to save my daughter's life on that fateful day, what would have helped? He replied "a Rotem machine."OK, you've got one", I hastily replied, not realising the enormity of the task I had just set myself.

(Bleeding after childbirth usually requires blood transfusion which may lead to increased morbidity and mortality. It is therefore important to appropriately treat the cause of the bleed and reduce the blood loss. Knowledge of the exact cause of the bleed allows treatment to be tailored rather than replacing blood loss with transfusion. The Rotem machine has been developed to monitor the clotting process and helps differentiate between clotting and bleeding.)

So on the first anniversary of my daughter's death I started fund raising, kicking it off with a Wing Walk. Probably fairly foolish, as I'm scared of heights, but my way of dealing with it on that day was to think I would be up in the sky, so nearer my daughter and if I didn't make it, then hopefully I'd be with her.

It's very strange, but losing a child, especially an adult child, puts a completely different perspective on life. Losing my parents was the right order of things, so at some point, to be expected. Losing Victoria was neither the right order, or to be expected. She was a healthy, fit, active 36 year old, who before her pregnancy played rugby and yet here she was, dead from childbirth.

It didn't make any sense, nothing made any sense and I'm not sure if it ever will do again. I am still trying to raise the money for a Rotem machine and have held a concert, sold items at auction and elsewhere and am soon to hold another concert.

Victoria did so much herself for charity....raising money for Help the Heroes, doing a London to Brighton bike ride among some of her achievements, it is only right that there should be something in which to commemorate her.

I am hoping to eventually set up a charity in her memory, but that takes an awful lot of work, which at the moment I'm not capable of doing and certainly not on my own.

A few months after Victoria died to try and heal my mind I started writing a Blog 'A Mothers Cry of Pain'. I also have a Facebook page under the same name. Victoria's death shook me to my very core and even as I write this the tears flow. I felt as if I was going mad, my head was in a complete turmoil. I couldn't think straight. I was having panic attacks, I was waking up at 3 every night (the hour she died). I thought my head was going to explode.

I thought if I wrote down my feelings, then I could look back on them and see how far I'd come....how far I'd progressed....after all, in a few months I'd be back to normal....wouldn't I?

How wrong was I? I never ever expected to have the emotions I've experienced. I now know I will never be normal again. My head is still in a complete turmoil, I still have panic attacks, I still wake at 3am most nights, I cry in supermarkets for no reason, I'm in constant pain, and I'm a complete mess. It's not getting easier.

I'm not new to death, or loss. I have lost 2 babies during pregnancy, both parents, aunts, uncles, friends, but Victoria's death is by far the most devastating and still brings me to my knees. I have tried to understand why and I'm beginning to understand a little more. You expect Grandparents to die. You expect parents to die.

The two babies that died in pregnancy occurred after traumatic events, one after a car accident, so accountable for, although extremely sad and no doubt contributed to my eventual mental health.

When Victoria was a baby, she suffered from croup which on several occasions resulted in a trip to hospital, until one of the regular ambulance drivers showed me exercises to do on her to relieve the mucus that was in her lungs.

Victoria had all the childhood illnesses, including mumps, measles and whooping cough, which I nursed her through, watching her like a hawk, to make sure she was alright. Each time I worried and wondered if she would make it safely through. She always did.

She eventually made it through to adulthood and left the nest; obviously as a mother you still worry about your children, but she was sensible and fit. She had made it.

Her life as a wife and eventual mother was starting and once I had recovered from shingles I would be able to rejoice and share. Life was looking good.

Two strange things happened before that fateful night. About two or three weeks before Victoria died, I was sat on my bed, when over in the corner of my bedroom a rectangular framed picture appeared, ghost-like. It was my son-in-law to the right of the picture, me to the left and a little girl in the middle. I instinctively knew what it meant and shouted at the picture "NO, go away, I don't want to know". Was I right? Was I being prepared for what was to come, a premonition? I'm not sure, I have so many unanswered questions.

The second thing that happened was on that fateful night, the chest pain I was experiencing coincided with the timing of two of her heart attacks. I had asked the hospital for a minute by minute breakdown of everything that happened on that night from the moment she was admitted to hospital.

They sent it, and as I went through the timings, I realised that she had one heart attack, they resuscitated her, but she immediately went into a second heart attack. The timing of her two first heart attacks coincided with my chest pains. Did we connect in some way? Was she trying to contact me? I don't know. In all she had 4 heart attacks and they never managed to stop the bleeding. Reading the detailed notes, all hell broke loose in the operating theatre that night.

Victoria's death has changed everything, how could it not....how could any of us who knew her ever be the same again. For me, her death was so primal. The daughter I gave birth to died giving birth to her daughter.

Losing Victoria, has changed my view of death, I'm not scared of dying. My health has deteriorated since her death, as happens to so many parents who lose a child.

Three and a half years later and I still struggle on a daily basis. I've become very forgetful and paperwork, including important 'to do' things have accumulated on my study floor. I'm permanently tired. In short, I'm not functioning as a person. I wish I could get some of the images out my head.

Due to an autopsy, her cremation was delayed, which meant I was able to attend, as I was no longer infectious. The sight of her coffin coming out of the hearse still haunts me and if it hadn't been for my brother, who had come over from Australia, literally holding me up, I would have fallen to the floor. No parent wants to see the coffin containing their child....it's literally heart-breaking.

There are many times since Victoria's death when I've thought "I can't do this anymore" and days when I go to bed saying to God, "Don't wake me up in the morning", but He always does. There are still days when I want to scream "My daughter's dead", but I hang on as I have a job to do. I am the only living person who can tell my little Granddaughter what her mummy was like from birth. I want her to know what a beautiful person her mummy was. How she was loved so much.

The saddest thing is that my little Granddaughter will have heard her mummy's voice for nine months and then nothing. How did she process that? How does she process that? She never got to be held by her mummy and my daughter never got to hold her baby. How incredibly sad and unfair.

I've even questioned my relationship with God, I've certainly sworn at Him, but strangely, I never lost my faith. I know one day I'll see my daughter again and with each day that passes, that day comes just a little closer. And of course there's the Rotem machine that will be her legacy to prevent other mothers' daughters dying. It is for this reason that I am trying to raise money for a Rotem machine in her name, for Cheltenham and Gloucester Hospital where her daughter was born, but she sadly died.

JONATHAN
1979

"I don't know whether I have a legacy that you're looking for in your book" said Joy when we were discussing my project at a bereaved parents meeting called by her in the parish she served. So began a very different journey I had anticipated when I was looking for stories of how the creation of a legacy in memory of their child who had died emerged from a parent on the pathway through grief.

Instead of some of the traditional yet amazing examples contained in this book portraying tangible projects and fundraising, leaving an indelible mark on many people I found myself moved by how the loss of her son Jonathan changed the direction in her own life which, in itself, became a legacy benefiting many people.

There are dictionary definitions for legacy such as bequest and gift given in asset form so surely, I thought, if Joy's life had fundamentally changed which resulted in benefits to others then that change was just as much a gift. This then is Joy's story but also Jonathan's as he is imbedded into her life as much now as if he had survived and still lives.

I'm not sure that I have created a legacy for grief. I haven't set up a charity, or sponsored a child in a Third World country, or done anything as tangible as that but this is an account of my life journey since the death of my baby son in 1979.

My first child, a girl, was born in 1975 after a straightforward pregnancy and birth. I did have to have a D and C 6 weeks after she was born as not all the placenta had come away but that was minor at the time. I became pregnant again at the beginning of 1979. This pregnancy was not straightforward. I started bleeding at 12 weeks and was given injections to secure the pregnancy. These didn't stop the bleeding and an ultrasound scan revealed placenta-previa. My GP, who was amazing in his support and help, ordered rest – no housework, no strenuous activity, on the understanding that if I hoovered the floor and then lost the baby, I would feel it was my fault. So, it was feet-up from June to August. I am so grateful to my GP and Health Visitor for all their support at the time. Fortunately, my then husband was a teacher, and this coincided with school holidays and we were also entitled to a home-help.

However, this didn't save the pregnancy and I went into labour at the end of August as the baby had died in utero from starvation. I was given a general anaesthetic but didn't need a caesarean section and I only know the baby was a boy because the medical staff told me. I never saw him. I was devastated.

As a Lay Worker for the Methodist Church and having had a breakdown from depression 2 years earlier I was determined not to go under with grief. My daughter was old enough to start school that September and so I went back to work and made a study of the bereavement process so I could understand what was happening to me. I was running a Parent and Toddler Group and over the following years until I left Bath, we had several miscarriages, stillbirths and neo-natal deaths among the parents who came to the group. Through our combined experiences I started to come to terms with my own loss.

People would ask me when I was going to become pregnant again but I didn't want to. I was scared it would happen again and my over-analytical mind said I would feel cheated if the next baby was another girl and if it was a boy, he would be in danger of replacing the son I had lost. It was years later that I realised I didn't want another child – I wanted, and still want the one I have lost.

My GP continued to support me and said the only reason for being pregnant was because I wanted to be pregnant not because I thought I should provide my daughter with a sibling or my parents with a grandchild. My husband felt the same and so we decided to stay with the lovely daughter we have and be grateful for her.

And so, my life moved on. I became more involved in pastoral care through the church, particularly with people who were depressed or bereaved. In 1986 I felt God was asking more of me and that it was right to move toward ordination in the Methodist ministry. I started training to be a Methodist Local Preacher, but this didn't last long. The marriage I was in was unhappy. We had moved from Bath and I decided on a divorce.

I met my current husband in the Methodist Church but we had to leave it because the minister took exception to our relationship. We joined the local Anglican Church but I had to give up all ideas of being ordained because at that time there was no way I could become an Anglican priest as a divorced and remarried woman. So I concentrated on building a new marriage and looking after my daughter. In 1996, when the previous rulings about ordination had changed, I felt God was again calling me to ordained ministry. This was tested by the church. I started the training and was ordained in 2002.

I don't know how my life would have panned out if my son had lived. I can't put his death and my ordination on a pair of scales so they balance each other. All I know is that his death has led to me becoming a priest.

In these last 17 years as a priest I have encountered people whose babies and children have died. My own experience, now 40 years on, I think has enabled me to be empathic and supportive of others. I still grieve for the son I haven't brought up to adulthood, but I am touched by the opportunities I have to be alongside those who have similar losses. This is the legacy I have found, and I am grateful for it.

"CHON" ABBEY
1.2.1998 To 11.11.2016

In July 1998, Geoff and Jo Abbey moved to Bangkok, Thailand for a 3 year posting with Geoff's work. After the initial settling in period Jo started voluntary work at an orphanage in Bangkok called Baan Nor Giank – 'New Life'. The orphanage was privately owned which cared for a small number of orphans passed to their care from the state welfare system. A number of the children were either infected by HIV or given up to the state from families infected by the disease. The orphanage had some full time carers but mainly relied on volunteers and charity fundraising to manage the home. They cared, homed and provided medication for the babies throughout their early years of development and the transition into schools and education.

Jo would visit a couple of days a week to help where she could with the care of the babies. On one such visit the owner of the orphanage approached Jo and asked if she was willing to volunteer on a more regular basis as they were expecting the arrival of some new babies from the welfare system and more help would be appreciated. Jo had no hesitation in agreeing to help where she could. Later that same week a group of new babies arrived at the orphanage and Jo was immediately drawn to one of them, a small baby boy who was 6 months old. The Thai staff named this baby boy Chon which in Thai meant a body of water. Chon had been given up by his maternal family into the state welfare system several months earlier and although he was found not to have HIV, his family were infected by the disease and as such felt that he would have a better chance in life if they gave him up with the hope he would be eventually adopted into a new family.

Jo immediately fell in love with Chon who wore the brightest of eyes and warmest of smiles. Chon also fell in love with Jo and demanded her attention all the time and was reluctant to allow the other babies to share Jo's attention. Jo was the only person who could comfort him when he cried, the only person allowed to feed him, the only person allowed to play with him, the only person allowed to love him. Chon would be very distraught when Jo had to leave at the end of each day, crying at the window as Jo left. Jo herself found it too distressing as well leaving Chon there and would also share his distress when she returned home. Geoff would visit at weekends and time off from work and quickly fell in love with Chon as well and recognised the close bond that Jo and Chon had developed.

A few months after Chon had arrived at the orphanage Geoff and Jo started making enquiries into the possibility of adopting Chon as their own son. The orphanage gave their full support and blessing, allowing Chon to spend days with them away from the orphanage and on occasions overnight whilst they navigated their way through the adoption process. Eventually he was allowed to live permanently with Geoff and Jo where they were visited by child welfare officers to assess their suitability to become adoptive parents.

Finally, approximately 12 months after making those initial enquiries Geoff and Jo, with Chon sat on Jo's knees, they were interviewed by the Thai Welfare State's Child Adoption board and approval was given for them to formally adopt Chon as their own Son.

Chon was christened at the residence of HM Ambassadors to Thailand on Sunday 6th February 2000 and given the name Jonathan George Abbey although he was always known by his Thai nickname of Chon. British citizenship was granted in July 2000 and in January 2001 the Abbey's returned back to the UK to start their 'new lives'.

From being given up as an orphaned baby with the hope he would have a better life Chon was now part of a new family becoming a much loved Son, Grandson, Nephew and Cousin as well as an adored friend to so many.

Chon joined the Village Primary School in September of the same year and so began his love of the village and everyone who lived there. He quickly made friends with fellow classmates and this friendship remained strong throughout his life. Friendship was important to Chon – he did not care if they were cool kids or not, tall or short, thin or fat, he would always spend time with anyone, all he asked in return was the ability to share his love of life, the ability to laugh, joke and have fun.

He viewed the village as just one large playground whether it be on the school playing fields, the line-bank, or the footpaths through the village. Always with a big smile, a wave or a thumbs-up. He did not shy away from chatting to people young or old whether it be a quick 'hello' or 'alright' to a conversation about anything they wanted to talk about.

School and College was an unwelcome distraction although it was an opportunity to broaden his network of friends, of which there were many. The village playground extended into Brackley and beyond continuing with his simple philosophy of enjoying life.

Any tribute to Chon would not be complete without mentioning wheels! 1 wheel, 2, 3 & 4 wheels – basically if it had a wheel Chon would be using it. It started as a young child riding 3 wheel trikes around the Embassy grounds each morning and afternoon. One of his first words was 'car' and he could easily and excitedly point out different models of cars by the make badge. Teaching him to ride a bike without stabilisers at Garth Park in Bicester was relatively quick and easy and he was soon getting his parents to time him as he raced around the footpaths of the park, often drawing a small crowd who would encourage him to beat his previous time.

Birthdays and Christmas presents were simple as it would always involve a bigger and faster bike, a scooter or skateboard and then the unicycle which he quickly mastered the technique of riding. Footpaths around Helmdon were simply an improvised race track for him and his friends. Pieces of wood and timber from their garden shed were being used to make different types of ramps for him to launch himself into the air so he could perform tricks before landing further down the road. Geoff would regularly find himself at the end of the day clearing away the timber and leaving them at the side of the house so they could quickly be re-assembled the following day.

And of course there was the continual washing and cleaning of his vehicle, the 'lengthy' washing of his car in the lay-by outside their home plus the small rivers of soapy water running down the hill into the village – but this was not a sudden need to ensure his car was spotlessly clean, this had been going on for several years before. Often they would go into their back garden to discover a new water feature had been created by Chon after either washing his Motorbike or Scooter or BMX bike. Chon had other passions such as Photography, Golf and Karting all of which he was very good and accomplished at but cars and bikes were his real passion.

On Sunday 16th October 2016 Geoff and Jo drove Chon and his best friend, Ashley to London Heathrow Airport where they said an emotional goodbye to them both as they set off on their first 'trip of a lifetime'. Chon had completed his College studies in June earlier that year and had found employment in the Motorsport industry, an industry he wanted to work in. The plan was to visit Dubai for 5 days before travelling to Thailand, his country of birth. They were lucky enough to adopt Chon as their only child so as an 18 year old they were letting him go and explore the big wide world for himself with his best mate, experiencing its beauty and glory. As parents they were naturally nervous and anxious and made sure he was prepared for the world's not so beautiful and glorious wonders. They did, however, understand how important it was for Chon to make this journey. Anyway it was only for a month and he would be back home before they knew it. He would return a different boy, a young man, a little bit wiser and a little bit more mature. They did though shed a few tears saying goodbye.

On Friday 11th November 2016 Chon and Ashley were into the 2nd day of a 3 day motorcycle trip around Central Thailand. Chon was buzzing! They had seen and done Dubai, visited Bangkok and explored the Islands in Southern Thailand. Having returned to Bangkok they were into the final stages of their trip, only 5 more days and they would return back to the UK. Geoff and Jo were counting the days.

On the afternoon of that Friday they were given the news that all parents fear and turned their life into a living nightmare; their beloved son, Chon, the centre of their world had tragically died in a road traffic accident. The country that had given up on him 18 years previously had now taken him back instantly whilst he was enjoying life to the full, at his happiest, with his life ahead of him and all set to embrace it.

Geoff and Jo were living in every parent's worst fear. They were thrown into a new life they did not seek and certainly did not welcome. Their child had died and they were still living in this world without him. Their lives were filled with complete heartache.

They have found since the accident they gained comfort from writing about Chon and his life. It helps them feel that he is still alive. He will always be a massive part of their lives, will always be by their side and he of course will always be loved. By sharing their stories of Chon and their experiences they hope to give some comfort and help to others who are enduring the same pain and heartache as well as giving some comfort, help and occasional advice to those considering adopting an orphaned child.

It is still very raw for them and they understand that they will never recover from this or may never be truly happy again but writing blogs and stories will help heal the wound though the scar will remain forever. They told Chon about the world before he departed on his trip of a lifetime – now they feel it's time to tell the world about Chon.

They have been using Chon's memory and infectious love of life to support a children's orphanage in Thailand. They were incredibly blessed to have adopted Chon from the Baan Nor Giank Children's Orphanage located in Bangkok in 1999. Unfortunately they discovered that the orphanage no longer operates as the owner and founder retired.

They did visit the grounds of Baan Nor Giank during their visit to Thailand and the current occupiers allowed them to hang an orchid on a tree in the garden in Chon's memory and assured them they would care and nurture the plant on their behalf.

They discovered another privately funded Children's Orphanage located in Lopburi, Central Thailand that shared the same values and aims as Baan Nor Giank. After meeting with the Children's Rights Foundation in Bangkok and listening to the work they do in caring and loving orphaned children who have been affected by either HIV, drugs abuse or abandonment they made the decision to support Baan Gerda Children's Orphanage by raising funds through events and making donations directly to the Orphanage.

Baan Gerda currently cares for over 85 children at their location just north of Lopburi. Ironically the monkey temple Chon and Ash visited on the 11th November 2016 is also located in Lopburi.

The monies raised will be used to provide medical care and medicines, clothing, food, education plus school equipment as well as day to day running costs of the orphanage. As with many such orphanages they do rely on donations and support to continue their work ensuring the children receive the right level of care and love all children so rightly deserve. Unfortunately the problem of orphaned children in Thailand does not stop and whilst some of the privately owned orphanages receive some government funding for particular medicines they do rely heavily on funding and donations. Without this funding the orphanages would simply be unable to continue to operate in providing care and support to the children and they would be left extremely vulnerable.

It is personally sad for Geoff and Jo that Baan Nor Giank no longer operates with so many personal memories from their time visiting and supporting the orphanage thereby allowing them to adopt Chon as their only child. However, they accept their decision to support Baan Gerda, thereby creating the legacy in Chon's name they wished for. They have also been assured they will receive regular updates on how the money is being used which they will publish for all to see.

Through events held in 2017 they were able to donate to Baan Gerda approximately £8,000 which is already making a difference to the lives of all the children. They added to that figure in 2018 which continues to give children similar opportunities to Chon and a love of life and will have achieved their hope of building a legacy in Chon's name.

They recognise the kind generosity given in Chon's memory such as individual donations on the day of his service and through Humphri's just giving page; Beth Bruce organising the Magdalen College School Brackley mufti-day event that was recognised as one of the best contributed charity collections they have had; Kurtis Butler, Michael O'Brien and of course Ash Valentine organising Chon's Memorial Trophy karting race in February, which will be repeated each year as it has already generated much interest from many wishing to take part; Chon's work colleagues at Progressive Motorsport Ltd who made a very generous single donation in his memory; and his village community in Helmdon who organised a Christmas Lunchtime event in the Reading Room; for all these they have been able to transfer across to Baan Gerda a total of £4,900. His primary school in Helmdon have also created a new award for their end of year awards ceremony. The Chon Abbey Memorial award is awarded to the year 6 pupil who is considered the most 'kindest and friendliest' pupil in their year group which reflects some of Chon's qualities that he will be most remembered for. Although there are no funds raised through this it is hoped that the award will continue for years to come ensuring that he will always be remembered by the school.

They have continued to raise monies through other events and sponsorship including a 3 peak challenge in 2018 for Baan Gerda as well as setting up their own just giving page to allow them to create a legacy in Chon's name, one that they will be proud to support and take comfort from and one that they know Chon will be proud of.

THOMAS THEYER
7.6.1995 to 19.7.2013

Thomas was born at 5.38 pm on June 7th, 1995, he was born equipped to run, with long legs! He measured 56 cm in length. He was a beautiful child, big brown eyes, with long lashes. From the day he was born we adored him. He loved Tigger from Winnie the Pooh and we would say – give us a 'Tigger'.

Thomas was an easy child, he was loving, happy, never angry, and never unkind. Not long after he started primary school, I received a telephone call requesting me to attend the school to see the headmistress to talk about Thomas. I remember clearly being sat in her office and her asking me if we had come to terms with Thomas's autism. I had no idea what she was talking about and in hindsight I don't think she did. That may sound bitter, but I think people label very quickly. His class teacher was wonderful, she had an interest in special educational needs and went on to become a Special Educational Needs Coordinator. When I spoke to her she said that she had noticed that Thomas had difficulty following multiple instructions, her example was that at break time she had told the children to go to the cloakroom, put on their hats and coats and go out to play, but Thomas only got as far as the cloakroom. Thomas went through a series of assessments, including being tested for Petit Mal (now called absence seizures) and ultimately he was diagnosed as having Attention Deficit Disorder (ADD) and Dyspraxia. He had a full statement of Special Educational Needs (SEN) throughout his schooling and maximum teaching support hours.

I remember taking Thomas to school and watching him shuffle around in the playground on his own, I would go home and cry at the thought of him being so isolated. There were incidents of cruelty, one child put a knife to his neck in the queue for lunch (a blunt dinner knife), at secondary school he was called the freak by another boy and when Aimee his sister went to the same school, a child came up to her and said 'so you're the freaks sister'. These incidents were however not frequent though they hurt. His secondary school was fantastic, any issues were resolved quickly and Thomas loved the school. Overall, he was well liked. I feel that the world is becoming more accepting of the differences in others, or at least, I hope so.

We live in the beautiful Peak District of Derbyshire and have wonderful countryside to enjoy and as a family we walked every week. When Thomas was 15, I telephoned the local athletics club to see if he could join the juniors. The club welcomed Thomas. He ran with the juniors every Monday and Thursday evening and the club became a massive part of his life. The highlight of his year was the club's annual road race held on Carnival day. Thomas first ran this race when he was 15. The race is now held in Thomas's memory every year.

The summer Thomas died should have been so special, Aimee had finished her GCSEs, had her prom and Thomas was 18 on June 7th. The day after Thomas's birthday we went to Kefalonia for our last ever family holiday. When we came back Thomas ran in another local race, the Whaley Waltz Fell race on June 29th and then the carnival race, the 'Carnival 4' on July 13th. His race number for the Whaley Waltz was 95, the year he was born, and his race number for the Carnival 4 was

123. He died 6 days after the carnival race, on Friday 19th July 2013. I remember thinking, 123 and he was gone.

The day Thomas died our world changed forever. A bereaved parent knows the pain and the endless yearning for their child, the total confusion that he/she is not there. It is almost too painful now to talk about Thomas's death, and for us, too complicated. I just know that I woke up one sunny day in July, and when I went to bed that night, with the help of sedatives, my son, my beautiful, kind wonderful son was dead. I believe bereaved parents share a foundation of pain but on top of that we all have our own layers of horror, the things that keep us awake at night. My layers include that Thomas died on his own, that he might have called out for me, that he felt fear, that he felt pain, but above all that he was alone. To read in the post mortem report his injuries and how he was found left me reeling. I found myself many times on my knees in desperation, in tears, as if to stay standing was just too hard.

We received many cards and messages; the church was full at Thomas's funeral and several people spoke, they all spoke of his kindness, goodness, and humour. I spoke about the Thomas we loved so much and some of the things he did, because he just saw things differently. I also spoke of his love and kindness. He was 6 foot 3, my son, my beautiful tall boy, I remember saying that I used to put my arms round him and my head would be on his chest and I couldn't believe I was never going to be able to do that again. To not be able to speak, hold or see your child again, is a torture.

I looked for Thomas in the early days, weeks, and months after he died. I turned up at a friend's house and said I couldn't find him. I felt like I was losing my mind. When I was alone, in the places we walked, I screamed his name.

Someone, I had once met through work sent me an e-mail in which he told me about the loss of his daughter. He said, 'it tears you apart', how true he was. It tore us apart, my husband, myself, and our daughter we fell to pieces each in different ways. I collapsed, for months, I went from the bedroom to the couch, lost nearly 2 stone in weight and could not go out. The doctor put me on different anti-depressants, eventually I gave up on them as they either left me unable to do anything or running round in a kind of manic state.

Once I did start to go out, just to do simple things like the shopping, I turned right when I left our house, not left. I went in the opposite direction from where I knew people and places. I went to where I could be as anonymous as possible. I bumped the car 2 or 3 times. A friend described me as broken. Thomas filled my head. Some days I would stare at the digital photo frame we had, at picture after picture of Thomas and us, smiling, happy, and the tears just ran endlessly down my face. Other times I couldn't look at the photo frame. I shut the door to his bedroom and couldn't go in, but every night outside his room I said goodnight Tompy, I love you. Alan, my husband, grew a beard, and people would walk past him in the street and not recognise him. He liked it that way and carried on working. He filled every minute, when he wasn't working, he was walking, running, bike riding or swimming. He could not stand it when I cried and would shut the door. My pain, on top of his, was too much to take. We came close to breaking and there were times when I thought we would part.

Alan was always a great dad, always having fun with the children. Seven years on and we turn to each other when we feel the pain becoming too much, we are there for each other, but in the early days it was too much.

At times Aimee had been a mini mum to Thomas, looking out for him at school and she made sandwiches for his lunch the day before he died. Thomas loved Aimee very much. This picture of Thomas and Aimee was taken outside Aimee's prom just weeks before his death. Thomas had been running and came to see his sister outside the prom venue. It was a sunny evening, lots of happy faces everywhere and Thomas was excited to see all his old teachers again.

Aimee started six form in the September after Thomas died. I look back and think how hard that must have been for her. Sometimes she would get into college and then I would get a phone call to pick her up. She struggled with anxiety and panic attacks and pretty much missed fifty percent of year 1. She is now 23. Thomas has been dead 7 years – he is now 25. That's what I say to people. I say is, not would have been. I know he's dead, but I just can't do 'would have been'.

I visit the cemetery regularly. On his birthday and the anniversary of his death I sit by his grave and write to him. I tell him our family news and about the wonderful things that have happened/are happening in the charity set up in his name.

From the beginning we wanted to do something good in Thomas's name and with the help of some truly kind and special friends the Thomas Theyer Foundation was set up. Our first event was a tabletop sale. We went on to hold other events and in June 2015 when we had raised £5,000.00, we became a registered charity.

Thomas loved swimming and running and we saw as a family how important this physical activity was for Thomas, how it helped his gross motor skills and the enjoyment he got from sports and outdoor activities which was a massive part of his life. Thomas once said if he won the lottery, he would give it all to charity. I said if he won the lottery perhaps we could have a little of the money, but he said no – it would all go to charity. Thomas didn't need money, he had us and he didn't want much. He was truly a gentle person. He stopped to talk to people when he was running. He was just good.

The Thomas Theyer Foundation's over-riding aim is to provide access to physical activity, for children and young people like Thomas and also children and young people who are experiencing difficult life circumstances. Over the last few years the charity has funded non-residential outdoor activities for its beneficiaries and is currently raising money to build a self-contained lodge at an outdoor centre in the Peak District of Derbyshire, so that children like Thomas can enjoy residential stays and respite breaks with their families.

In 2018 the charity opened its first Sports and Outdoor Charity shop and continues to promote the charity and its aims through this shop whilst also raising funds. In 2020 two successful funding applications were gained to start the charities counselling service for families, and it is looking for premises for a support centre. At the heart of everything we do is Thomas. We think about what helped Thomas and us, his family, the difficulties he and we faced during his life and as a result of his death.

My favourite quote is one I found by chance. It always reminds me of Thomas and I try to remember it every day and, as far as possible, live by it, even on those days when the pain of his loss feels too much to bear.

The true essence of humankind is kindness. There are other qualities which come from education or knowledge, but it is essential, if one wishes to be a genuine human being and impart satisfying meaning to one's existence, to have a good heart.

Tenzin Gyatso (1935)
The 14th Dalai Lama (B. 1935)

Thomas had such a good heart. His legacy is the Thomas Theyer Foundation. Some days it has given me a reason to get out of bed and everything we achieve is because of Thomas. The charity has now raised over £200,000.00

TOM OWEN
25.7.1995 to 30.1.2017

After a number of years of receiving fertility treatment, our dreams came true when we were blessed with a beautiful baby boy, our precious Tom.

Sadly, our world came crashing down when Tom was killed in an accident at work on 30 January 2017. Tom was electrocuted whilst working as an apprentice jointer for Western Power Distribution. He was just 21 and had his whole life ahead of him. A life that he loved.

When we talk about Tom now, we often think it sounds like we are remembering him through rose tinted glasses, maybe we are, but he truly was the perfect son. Our gentle giant with a kind and caring heart with a great sense of humour. He had the biggest smile which would light up a room and a wicked sense of humour. We are incredibly proud of the young man that he became.

Tom grew up in a small Welsh village and was a real home bird. He had a real passion for travel but he was always glad to come home. He enjoyed many trips of a lifetime in his short life including Canada, South Africa, Maldives, Bali and Ecuador. A very clear memory we have of Tom at 16 was during a family holiday to South Africa when he insisted on pushing his Granny around the top of Table Mountain in a wheelchair rather than her missing out. It's just as well he was a big strong lad!

Tom's expedition to Ecuador had a defining influence on him too. He worked on a project in the Amazon where he saw so much poverty, it really changed his perspective on life. He returned from that journey a different person and had grown up so much in a relatively short space of time. He had so many more plans to travel to other wonderful places, so many hopes, dreams and aspirations.

Tom's other passion was sport. He played roller hockey for Wales U10s when he was 7 years old but sadly had to give it up because of competing priorities with his rugby. Tom absolutely loved rugby. He started playing at 6 years old and played for every age group and team at our local rugby club, his beloved Beddau RFC. As a big lad he was always "destined" to be a forward and plied most of his trade in the front row. Tom was a promising rugby player and even got called up to play for the 1st XV whilst he was Youth player. Quite an accomplishment as a 17 year old playing for a premiership level team. Tom was a loyal and faithful servant to his club and one of his coaches has remarked that he was green and gold to the core (club colours)!

Tom was also an accomplished golfer. He enjoyed the game recreationally with his friends and as a member of the local golf club. He was the proud owner of a number of trophies.

Whenever we discussed the possibility of Tom moving away when he left home, he always said "Why would I? I have everything here; my family, my friends and the rugby club and golf club"! He even said that if he went to University he would stay local.

In the end, he chose to pursue an apprenticeship with Western Power Distribution rather than go to university. On the day that we delivered Tom to the training centre in Taunton we never for one minute imagined how it would end. As always we were so proud of what he had achieved. We can't say too much about the circumstances of Tom's death as it's still subject to investigation, except that we still have a long and hard journey ahead of us to get justice for our son.

So, roll forward to 30 January 2017. When we got up for work that day little did we know that our lives would be changed completely, forever. It's hard to understand how life can go on but it does; daily routine helps. More importantly, the love and support that we have received from a very close community and some very good friends has got us through. Tom proved that he was very good at picking his friends – they have and continue to be there for us every step of the way as we have tried to re-build our lives.

We realised after Tom's death that we needed to find something positive to focus on during our darkest days and to help take us forward. Initially we had chosen a small local charity, Follow Your Dreams, to receive donations in Tom's memory instead of floral tributes. The charity supports children and young people with learning disabilities and their families to help them achieve their dreams. This may include something as simple as learning to swim or play an instrument through to learning life skills and gaining work experience. We subsequently decided to 'adopt' the charity and to continue to raise funds for them as a legacy to Tom so that some good could come from his death. Helping young people to follow their dreams, because he can't follow his dreams.

We've raised the money in lots of ways but with particular support from our local rugby club and community. The support we have received from the local community and the club has been beyond measure. Tom's sister Katie, who was 15 when we lost Tom, has played in a charity rugby match organised by the ladies at the club, Beddau Pink Bulldogs, and she had never played before! She was honoured to wear Tom's number during the game. She has since taken up playing the game regularly – not sure what her brother would make of that! Katie also completed the Welsh 3 Peaks Challenge with Tom's best friends in just over 16 hours on what would have been his 22 birthday. We've held auctions, raffled rugby tickets, friends have run half marathons and 10k races and so much more. Last year, Katie and boys did a sky dive in Swansea on his birthday raising over £2k.

So far we have raised over £30k for Follow Your Dreams which they have used to help fund workshops and events. It is hoped that they will be running a rugby camp for disabled children in Tom's memory. He would love that!

The plan this year was for them to tackle the UK Three Peaks Challenge but unfortunately COVID19 has prevented that for the time being. Hopefully they will be able to do it this year and then we will have to think of the next challenge! Maybe they could do a bungee jump? Tom would be impressed with that. He bungeed off the Soweto Towers himself.

Whatever we do it will always be difficult without Tom but we will always do it with him in our hearts and to keep his memory alive. Tom was an incredibly special person and touched so many lives, more than we ever realised, and he will continue to make a difference. He will continue to give Katie a purpose too as she always says that she is living for two. As a big brother, he would be so proud of her.

DARREN SHAHLAVI
5.8.1972 to 14.1.2015

Darren was born in August 1972 in Stockport, Cheshire, the oldest of
my three children. Darren was always the quiet shy child with less
confidence than his siblings Bobby and Liz, so it was a surprise that he
grew up to be a martial arts actor eventually living in Hollywood. But
there were always other sides to Darren's character such as the more
public side; a confident martial artist, actor, story teller and bubbly
friend and also a deeper, quieter side to Darren's personality that
contributed to him being the gentle, caring and sincere person that he is

now recognised as: loving to his family and concerned about them; loyal to his friends; dedicated and hard working in his profession and generous to his fans who he always had time for.

Darren went to Hulme Hall School in Cheadle Hulme and it was there that he joined the gymnastic club. He was flexible, strong and agile and earned himself the best gymnast trophy in his final year. He also took part in acting at his school which gave him the chance to experience being on stage which he loved. These experiences helped him to become more confident and he was proud of these achievements. He gained a realisation that there were things he really enjoyed and was especially good at.

Darren loved learning Judo and Karate. He enjoyed martial arts not only for physical exercise and self-defence; he also learned about the discipline and moral elements of martial art as a way to conduct himself in life and this helped to further shape his personality, his communication and his style of connecting to people which was one of respect and gratitude.

Darren loved to study martial arts films and watch his heroes such as Bruce Lee, Jackie Chan and Jean Claude Van-Damme who he acted with in two films (Kickboxer Retaliation and Pound of Flesh) both sadly released after his death. Darren was also inspired by Donnie Yen who he later acted alongside in the film Ip Man 2.

Darren left home at the age of 18 to live and work abroad firstly in Malaysia then Hong Kong and Canada and his final destination, Hollywood, USA. Darren loved his family and missed us as much as we missed him. He travelled home as often as he could and spent his last Christmas with us in 2014 and returned to the USA just two weeks before his death. We had a wonderful time together and his family will treasure these last memories of him especially the fun that he had with his little niece Millie and nephew Leo.

Darren had a dream, a teenage ambition to reach Hollywood and become a respected and talented actor. He achieved that ambition whilst at the same time remaining a grounded individual, and a loving and much loved family member and friend.

The films he acted in have become Darren's own legacy and his family have been touched by the many tributes that came from his fans as well as other actors, directors, stunt coordinators and film crews. The films he was in involved martial arts and appealed to a certain sector of young males, some of whom had a life of struggle and felt inspired by him to train, keep fit and emulate his dedication and determination and to overcome obstacles and follow their dreams, whatever those may be.

Darren worked hard at maintaining physical fitness, agility and muscle strength. He went to the gym daily and ate a healthy, balanced diet. It was a great shock to his family and all who knew Darren when he died suddenly on 14th January 2015 of a heart attack caused by atherosclerosis, a silent killer that had been progressing for years unknown and undetected.

Darren's family soon realised that if he had been screened when he was younger then he might still be alive today so we turned our attention to raising funds for Cardiac Risk in the Young. In her legacy to her brother, Darren's sister Liz organised a 'Christmas in Hollywood' charity ball and with money raised, 80 young people have been screened. We believe that if just one person's life was saved the fundraising would be worthwhile.

As his mother I have naturally been devastated by my son's death. I have been helped considerably by The Compassionate Friends, a charity for bereaved parents, siblings and grandparents. Reflecting on my son's death and the pain I feel has also involved thinking about his future and I fear that as a childless man Darren's memory will eventually fade, even within the family. My legacy to him is a book I am preparing, not for publication or general consumption. It is a photo book that I am having printed with photos and the story of his life to give to his nieces and nephews to keep their Uncle's memory alive and keep the stories about him alive for future generations of the family. Darren has a niece and nephew, Millie and Leo who were only 6 and 10 when he died and their memories of him are limited. He also has a nephew and niece, Luccini and Capri, who never saw him because they were born after his death. My 'Darren' book will be a legacy for the existing family and future generations, a story of the uncle that should have been in their lives, who was full of love and fun and whose memory I want to keep alive through stories and photographs; a book that each of them will have to keep, to share with their children and grandchildren, a book about their wonderful Uncle Darren, my dear son.

GEORGI HICKMAN
20.9.1992 to 5.4.2017

We lost our daughter Georgi, aged 24, just over 3 years ago due to a series of catastrophic events following a reaction to nuts.

Georgi was a bright, fun and hugely loving person who shone through so many lives. The Big Issue Foundation was a cause that was very close to her heart. She would often spend time on nights out chatting to the homeless and making sure that their voices were heard.

Instead of flowers at her funeral, we asked for donations to the Big Issue and to celebrate her birthday each year we have now held 3 events that have been a lovely afternoon in a pub garden, with live music, food, games, etc. We have also hosted 2 quiz nights and took part in a sponsored Big Issue sleep out in a football stadium. In March '19 we walked through the night in London in The Big Issue sponsored night walk and also in April last year, her boyfriend ran the London marathon for her. We have so far raised about £23,500 which includes the £3000 target that was set for the marathon and subsequently doubled by his generous employers. The Covid-19 situation has prevented us from hosting any events this year but we intend to keep fundraising for the homeless in the future. It helps keep Georgi's memory alive and gathers all who love and miss her together, something she would love to see.

Our darling girl is sorely missed, but supporting The Big Issue will help ensure that her desire to help the homeless continues.

REUBEN GRAHAM
10.9.2010 to 21.8.2012

I do believe that we all have the ability to leave this world a better place than how we found it. Allow me to introduce you to my story. We'd already had our holidays that year, but still managed to sneak off to Devon with friends and family for a short break, camping. On one of the days, we all went out to a little amusement park.

Reuben had a great time. He was with his cousins, his big brother and his friend Callum. He took to the rides and went through the maze, he climbed on the outdoor equipment and panned for gold. He gave Sam a high five as Sam hit his first hole-in-one on the crazy golf. That evening, we all headed back for a barbecue. Reuben still had his appetite and, if I'm honest, he probably ate one too many sausages, as he paraded around the garden shouting, "sausage, sausage... Mmmmm, sausage..."

After I'd put Reuben to bed, we were still in the garden and Reuben had by then settled down to sleep, or so we thought. From inside our tent came a barrage of song; "Oh na na what's my name? Oh na na what's my name?"

We all started laughing but for Mike and I this was nothing out of the ordinary. If Reuben couldn't sleep he would often burst into song and sometimes this could go on intermittently for a couple of hours. Next, he started humming his favourite holiday song from Turkey. This was to be our final night with our boy.

Reuben slept really well that night and we were woken by the seagulls squawking around us. Reuben turned over in his travel cot and looked at me. "Morning mummy," he smiled.

"Come on," I said, "you fancy a cuddle?"

He piled into our bed and Isaac dived in too. There had been a lot of this going on in our house for quite a few months and even on work days we all managed to squeeze in some cuddle time. Just a couple of weeks prior to this, I had stopped in my tracks to think about how lucky we were to have such lovely moments of pure 'cuddledom'. I told myself that these were moments I should cherish, as soon my boys would be too big for cuddles. "Give me a kiss Reuben," I said.

"No!"

"Give me a kiss or I will tickle you"

"No, yes, no, yes... Daddy," he said, "kisssssss" *What a monkey!!!!* He was playing us off against each other for kisses. We were running out of time and had no idea ......

A week later, our darling, gorgeous, cheeky, funny little Reuben passed away in my arms. He had a brain tumour, it was stealth, it took him within a week of it being found and later we were to find that the tumour was rare, aggressive, cancerous and only 6-8 weeks old.

I lay him on the bed and promised him that his life would not be in vain and that we would make a little piece of the world better in his memory and name...

2 days later we launched his legacy "Reuben's Retreat".

I decided we would create a sanctuary for families facing an uncertain future with complex poorly children. A place where they could visit, take a break, a place to relax and recharge. It would also be a place for parents of loss, like us, a place to remember and rebuild.

The charity goes from strength to strength and I feel really honoured and blessed to walk with my angel Son every day, hand in hand, to deliver his legacy.

Reuben passed aged 23 months and less than 3 weeks later we were due to travel with his God Mothers to Center Parcs to celebrate his 2nd birthday. Chosen as a traffic free destination, to allow his independence to thrive and for him to have the freedom to go where he wanted with his big Brother.

The night before we left, my heart was broken, I couldn't pack for him, even the house hurt for him, as we were all so desperately grieving for our boy. I wanted to do something for him and I wrote this...

Reuben ~ by Mummy

You gave the bestest cuddles the best I've ever known.
They were so very special Reuben because they were home grown.
You'd wrap yourself round tightly and nuzzle into my cheek.
I'd kiss your curls and squeeze you tight and then I'd take a peek
to see if you would carry on or gently pull away
for Mummy didn't steal just one but many every day.
For I was the lucky one to have you as my son
and now I'm left here weeping for you have sadly gone
I ache for you my darling, my world is not the same.
I wish that things were different so you'd be in my arms again.
But now I have to carry on without you here to touch.
My heart breaks every day because I love you so very much
I hope that you can see us wherever you may be
and I hope that you tell all your friends about Isaac, Daddy and me.
And how your life was perfect, so happy and pure
and even if we tried real hard we couldn't love you more.
For we cannot see you Reuben or hear you speak our names.
We cannot watch you learn and grow and play your favourite games.
Although we have the memories to keep us warm at night
we wished we had you here dear Reuben to hold you very tight.
To kiss your curls and read you tales of knights so tough and bold
And tuck you up tight in your cot to stop you getting cold.
But you are gone and we are here, the memories we hold very dear.
Your cheesy grin, your big brown eyes, your cheeky ways, your big high 5's.

Good night Reuben and until we are together,
we'll keep you tucked up safe and warm In our hearts and minds forever
Mummy xxxxxx

We lost Reuben in August 2012. Being a bereaved Mum has taught me so much. Delivering his angel work has taught me even more. Reuben walks with me every day. I have complete trust in his journey and I have made peace with my grief. It is love and that is why it is so painful. It takes a long time, although time doesn't heal and I don't particularly like that saying. Time gives you the distance for your grief to change shape. I also know and understand that no two people grieve the same, how can they. I know what it feels like to have a community of generous and kind souls lift you. I have learned that life can have purpose, even when you are hurting. Pain has taught me compassion, empathy and a desire to help others that walk this path. My resilience comes from a tenacity to find meaning in my story, Reuben's journey. I also know that people are, and have the ability to be amazing human beings, we are touched by generous souls every single day.

Our vision at Reuben's Retreat is to walk side-by-side, offering emotional and practical support to families bereaved of a child or those that have a life limited/ threatened child and may face an uncertain future. Enabling them to create memories cocooned in the sanctuary of Reuben's Retreat underpinned by our army of love and compassionate hearts.

We are many years into the journey now. We raised sufficient funds to buy an old cottage hospital in Derbyshire, amidst the rolling hills. It is 130 years old and we "raise to renovate" and are underway with an ambitious 10 phase renovation plan. The more we raise, the more we renovate, the more we renovate the bigger our offering to families.

We have managed to make a positive difference to hundreds of families, with many more to come. I don't think we ever expected our small, grassroots, organic, family charity to be the cause it is today. It is much needed and we remain grounded in our gratitude.

We all have the ability to leave the world a better place than we found it. One day at a time, we are sure doing that, in memory of a gorgeous little boy with a cheesy grin and a whole lot of love to give.

Thank you for reading our story; www.reubensretreat.org

THE COMPASSIONATE FRIENDS/CARDIAC RISK IN THE YOUNG

The Compassionate Friends (TCF) is a charitable organisation of bereaved parents, siblings and grandparents dedicated to the support and care of other similarly bereaved family members who have suffered the death of a child or children of any age and from any cause. Their objectives are primarily to advance and assist in mental and physical welfare following suffering and infirmity among (a) parents occasioned by the death of their child(ren) and (b) other close relatives of such child(ren), normally brothers, sisters and grandparents.

To promote and support research into and to publish the results of the search into medicine and road safety and other child life protection projects likely or intended effectively to reduce deaths among children.

To contact or donate: Head Office: Kilburn Grange, Priory Park Road, Kilburn, London NW6 7UJ Telephone 0345 1232304. Email: helpline@tcf.org.uk
Registered Charity No. 1082335

Cardiac Risk in the Young is a charitable organization whose aims are preventing young sudden cardiac deaths through awareness, screening and research, and supporting affected families. Every week in the UK at least 12 young people die of undiagnosed heart conditions. Since its formation in 1995, Cardiac Risk in the Young (CRY) has been working to reduce the frequency of young sudden cardiac death (YSCD). CRY supports young people diagnosed with potentially life-threatening cardiac conditions and offers bereavement support to families affected by YSCD. CRY promotes and develops heart screening programmes and funds medical research. CRY publishes and distributes medical information written by leading cardiologists for the general public. CRY funds specialist referral, screening and cardiac pathology services at leading UK hospitals.

To contact or donate: Head Office: Unit 1140B, The Axis Centre, Cleeve Road, Leatherhead, Surrey KT22 7RD. Telephone 01737 363222.
Email: cry@c-r-y.org.uk
Registered Charity No.1050845

Further copies of this book can be obtained from all good bookshops such as Waterstones and Amazon.

ACKNOWLEDGEMENTS

I would like to sincerely than all the parents who have contributed to this book. The stories of their beloved children and the many varied legacies created in their memory are truly inspiring. I would also like to thank Compassionate Friends and Cardiac Risk in the Young for all the help they have provided in bringing this book to fruition and to Caroline, David and Saskia at New Generation Publishing for their guidance through the process of finally getting this book out into the retail marketplace of Amazon, Waterstones and others.

It would be remiss of me also not to mention all the wonderful charities that have benefitted from the legacies created which are listed below. And finally, my thanks to my wife, Jane, who guided me in the right direction and gave me ideas to progress this book. Her inspiration and resilience following the loss of her own dear children Jenny and Adam always leaves me with the utmost admiration.

Andrew – TCF/CRY
Josh – The Christie Charitable Fund
Aiden – Aiden's Angels International/Mtitu Foundation
Megan – Ronald McDonald House Glasgow/ LoveOliver Charity
Dilly – Gloucester Academy of Music
Daniel – Anyone's Child Families for Safer Drug Control
Guy – Guy's Trust/ ActionAid/ Manta Watch
Charlie – Ride for Charlie/CRY
Debbie – Mary's Meals/Debbie Rooke Memorial Fund/TCF
Camilla – Cancer Support Scotland (Tak Tent)/ Random Acts of Kindness Foundation/ Jhamtse Gatsal Children's Community
George – Mental Health UK
Erif – Drugfam/TCF
Vicki – Breast Cancer Care/ Maggie's Centres/ Kicking off Against Cancer
Lucy – Nordoff Robbins/ Lucy Curran Memorial Fund
Will – Don't Forget the Donor/Will Houghton Foundation
Chon – Baan Gerda Children's Orphanage/ Chon Abbey Memorial Fund
Thomas – Thomas Theyer Foundation
Tom – Follow your Dreams
Darren - CRY
Georgi Hickman – The Big Issue
Reuben Graham – Reuben's Retreat

Lightning Source UK Ltd.
Milton Keynes UK
UKHW021313171220
375285UK00007B/179